Dear Mi   d

NATHY'S
KITCHEN

Delicious and Easy Recipes

Happy

Mothers

Day!

♥♥♥♥♥♥♥♥♥♥♥♥♥

Hazel

For John, who has tried everything in this book.
Thank you for doing the washing up.

NATHY'S KITCHEN

Delicious and Easy Recipes

NATHALIA TJANDRA

TRANSNATIONAL PRESS LONDON

2020

HERITAGE SERIES BY TRANSNATIONAL PRESS LONDON

Heritage Series 3

Nathy's Kitchen - Delicious and Easy Recipes

First Published in 2020 by TRANSNATIONAL PRESS LONDON in the United Kingdom, 12 Ridgeway Gardens, London, N6 5XR, UK.

www.tplondon.com

ISBN: 978-1-912997-39-8

Cover Design: Gizem Çakır
Cover Image and Interior Photos: Nathalia Tjandra

✱ CONTENTS ✱

SOUPS, APPETISERS & SALADS

04-25

SEA FOOD

28-46

CHICKEN

50-68

MEAT

72-90

NATHY'S KITCHEN
Delicious and Easy Recipes

PASTA, RICE & NOODLES
94-112

VEGETARIAN & VEGAN
116-134

DESSERTS & CAKES
138-145

HELLO!

My name is Nathalia Tjandra! My family and friends call me Nathy.

Welcome to my recipe book.

I was born and raised in Indonesia. I moved to the Netherlands when I was younger. I now work and live in the UK. I live in one of the most beautiful cities in the world, Edinburgh, with my husband, John.
I am an academic and a frequent traveller. I am also very passionate about cooking and photography. When I don't travel, I spend my weekends in the kitchen, creating and trying different recipes.
I find cooking very relaxing. I love cooking delicious, healthy but easy-to-make food. My recipes are influenced by my upbringing as well as my travelling experience. I hope you enjoy the recipes and have the chance to try them for your loved ones.

If you enjoy the recipes in this book, visit my Instagram page @nathys_kitchen or website https://www.nathyskitchen.com.

SOUPS, APPETISERS & SALADS

01

CHICKEN & LENTIL SOUP

PREP TIME
10 MINS

COOKING TIME
15 MINS

SERVING
2 PERSONS

DIFFICULTY
○ ✓ ○ ○ ○

INGREDIENTS

1 CHICKEN BREAST FILLET
1L WATER
SALT AND PEPPER
1 MEDIUM ONION, FINELY
CHOPPED
1 GARLIC CLOVE, MINCED
½ TBSP OF OLIVE OIL
100GR GREEN AND ORANGE
LENTIL
A HANDFUL OF SOYBEANS
A SMALL BUNCH OF PARSLEY

PREPARATION

Boil the chicken fillets with 1L water, season with salt and pepper. Remove the chicken, let them cool slightly, shred and set aside. In a large pan, sauté the onion and garlic with olive oil until fragrant and the onion is soft. Add the lentils and cover in oil. Add the chicken broth and cook until the lentils are soft. Add the soybeans and parsley. Cook for 2 mins more. Season to taste. Transfer to serving bowls and garnish with the shredded chicken.

02

ROAST RED PEPPER SOUP

PREP TIME
30 MINS

COOKING TIME
15 MINS

SERVING
4 PERSONS

DIFFICULTY
○ ✓ ○ ○ ○

INGREDIENTS

3 RED PEPPERS, HALVED
AND DE-SEEDED
3 GARLIC CLOVES, CRUSHED
2 TBSP OLIVE OIL
1 ONION, QUARTERED
1 TIN OF CHOPPED TOMATOES
450ML VEGETABLE STOCK
1 TSP SMOKED PAPRIKA
SALT AND PEPPER
A SMALL BUNCH OF PARSLEY,
CHOPPED

PREPARATION

Preheat the oven to 200C/gas 6. Arrange the red peppers and garlic in a baking tray, drizzle with 1 tbsp olive oil and season with salt and pepper. Roast for 30 mins until they are soft. In a large saucepan, sauté the onion with 1 tbsp olive oil for 5 mins. Stir in the chopped tomatoes and cook for 3 mins. Stir in the roast peppers and garlic and cook for further 5 mins. Season with the smoked paprika. Pour the stock into the saucepan. Let it boil and simmer for 3 minutes. Season to taste. Turn off the heat and blend the mixture using (hand) blender until smooth. Garnish with chopped parsley before serving.

03

CULLEN SKINK

PREP TIME
5 MINS

COOKING TIME
30 MINS

SERVING
2 PERSONS

DIFFICULTY
○ ⦸ ○ ○ ○

INGREDIENTS

1 TBSP BUTTER
1 MEDIUM ONION, CHOPPED
2 MEDIUM POTATOES, PEELED
AND CUT INTO 1CM CUBES
300ML WATER
250ML MILK
2 BAY LEAVES
2 SMOKED HADDOCK FILLETS
¼ - ½ TSP SMOKED PAPRIKA
A SMALL HANDFUL OF PARSLEY,
CHOPPED
SALT AND PEPPER

PREPARATION

Melt the butter in a saucepan over medium heat. Sauté the onion until soft. Add the potatoes and water and bring to boil. Simmer for 10-15 minutes.
In another pan, add the milk, bay leaves and haddock fillets. Cook for five minutes until just tender. Remove from the haddock and flake gently into large pieces.
Add the milk and flaked fish to the saucepan containing potatoes. Season with the smoked paprika, salt and pepper. Cook for a further 5 minutes. Remove the bay leaves. Remove from the heat and sprinkle with the chopped parsley.

04

AROMATIC CRISPY DUCK WITH PANCAKES

PREP TIME
10 MINS

COOKING TIME
1.5 HOURS

SERVING
4 PERSONS

DIFFICULTY
○ ⊘ ○ ○ ○

INGREDIENTS

1KG DUCK CROWN
1 TBSP SALT
2CM GINGER, GRATED
1 TBSP CHINESE FIVE-SPICE
24 PANCAKES, STEAMED
1 CUCUMBER, JULIENNED
5 SPRING ONIONS, JULIENNED
4-5 TBSP HOISIN SAUCE

PREPARATION

Preheat the oven to 170C/gas 3.
Rub the duck all over with salt. Then rub the duck with the grated ginger. Dust the duck with the Chinese five-spice. Roast the duck in the oven for 1.5 hours. Using a spoon, remove the fat from the skin a few times to make the duck crispy. Once the skin is golden and crispy, remove from the oven. Once the duck is slightly cool, remove the breast and sliced. Shred the rest of the meat using to forks. Serve with the steamed pancakes, cucumber, spring onion and hoisin sauce.

05

MARINADE

6 SHALLOTS, QUARTERED
4 GARLIC CLOVES
8 KEMIRI (CANDLENUTS), SLIGHTLY ROASTED
2 LARGE RED CHILLIES
2 TBSP PALM SUGAR
1 TBSP TAMARIND

2 TBSP GROUND CORIANDER
1 TBSP CUMIN
10 TBSP KECAP MANIS (SWEET SOY SAUCE)
SALT AND PEPPER
2 TBSP COOKING OIL
40 WOODEN SATAY SKEWERS

SWEET PORK SATAY (SATE BABI MANIS)

PREP TIME

20 MINS

COOKING TIME

MARINADE OVERNIGHT

SERVING

8 PERSONS

DIFFICULTY
○ ○ ✓ ○ ○

INGREDIENTS

1KG PORK STEAKS, CUT LENGTHWISE INTO 3-4 PARTS AND SLICE EACH PART THINLY

SAUCE
2 SHALLOTS, CHOPPED
2 GARLIC CLOVES
2 LIME LEAVES
1 TBSP SAMBAL OELEK
4 TBSP KECAP MANIS (SWEET SOY SAUCE)
½ TBSP COOKING OIL
½ LIME JUICE

PICKLE
2 LIME JUICE OR 2 TBSP VINEGAR
1-2 TSP SUGAR
1 CUCUMBER CUT INTO CHUNKS
2 SHALLOTS, CHOPPED
1 LARGE CHILLI, CHOPPED (OPTIONAL)
A PINCH OF SALT

PREPARATION

Put the sliced pork into a large bowl. Blend the marinating ingredients using a blender until smooth. Season to taste. Marinade the pork for at least 1 hour (better overnight). Soak the skewers in cold water for at least 30 mins to avoid burning when grilling. Thread the pork slices onto the skewers until about 10 - 15cm long. BBQ or grill the satays on a griddle pan (over medium heat) for 3-4 minutes on each side until they are cooked.

06

CORN FRITTER (DADAR JAGUNG)

PREP TIME
10 MINS

COOKING TIME
20 MINS

SERVING
4-6 PERSONS

DIFFICULTY
○ ⊘ ○ ○ ○

INGREDIENTS

500G SWEET CORN KERNELS OR FROZEN SWEET CORN, THAWED
3 EGGS, BEATEN
150G PLAIN FLOUR
3 GARLIC CLOVES, MINCED
3 SPRING ONIONS, CHOPPED
A HANDFUL OF CORIANDER LEAVES, CHOPPED
½ TBSP CHILLI FLAKES (ACCORDING TO TASTE)
SALT AND PEPPER
FRYING OIL
SAMBAL OR SWEET CHILLI SAUCE

PREPARATION

In a food processor, blend 200gr sweet corn. In a large bowl, mix the blended sweet corn, the rest of the sweet corn kernels, eggs, flour, garlic, spring onions, coriander leaves and chilli flakes. Season to taste. Heat the frying oil in a frying pan on medium-high heat. Once the oil is hot, drop a large spoonful of corn mixture carefully into the hot oil. Fry until the batter is golden brown (2-3 mins each side). Deep fry a few fritters at a time. Once they are cooked, scoop them up and drain on a wire rack or paper towel. Repeat the process until the batter is used up. Transfer them fritters into a plate. Serve with sambal or sweet chilli sauce.

07

PREPARATION

Boil the potatoes in salted water for ten minutes.

Rub the trouts with a drizzle of olive oil and a pinch of salt and paper. Place in a stainless-steel colander and cover with tin foil.

When the time is up on the potatoes, place colander directly over the pan of boiling potatoes. Turn the heat down to medium-low and cook for 8 to 10 minutes, or until the trouts and potatoes are cooked through.

Once cooked, remove the fish from the colander to a plate, and discard the skin. Drain the potatoes, and leave to steam dry for 1 minute, then tip back into the pan.

Mash the potatoes, spreading the mash around the sides of the pan to help it cool down quickly. When the potatoes are cooled, transfer to a bowl.

Flake the trouts into the bowl, add flour, egg, coriander leaves, spring onions, ground coriander, lemon juice and zest and salt and pepper. Mash and mix together well. Season to taste.

Dust a plate with a little flour. Divide the mixture into 10, then lightly shape and pat into circles about 2cm thick, dusting them with flour as you go. Put them onto a clean plate also dusted with a little flour.

Put them into the fridge for an hour before cooking – this will allow them to firm up slightly.

Heat some oil in a frying pan over medium heat, add the fishcakes and cook for 3 to 4 minutes on each side, or until crisp and golden. Serve right away with lemon and sweet chilli sauce.

HOMEMADE TROUT FISHCAKES

PREP TIME

30 MINS

COOKING TIME

30 MINS

SERVING

5 PERSONS

DIFFICULTY

○ ☑ ○ ○ ○

INGREDIENTS

4 MEDIUM POTATOES, CUT INTO CHUNKS

4 TROUT FILLETS, SKIN ON

A BUNCH OF CORIANDER LEAVES, CHOPPED

A BUNCH OF SPRING ONIONS, CHOPPED

1 TBSP CHILLI FLAKES (ACCORDING TO TASTE)

1 TBSP GROUND CORIANDER

1 LARGE EGG

½ LEMON JUICE AND ZEST

4 TBSP PLAIN FLOUR, PLUS EXTRA FOR DUSTING

SALT AND PEPPER

SWEET CHILLI SAUCE

1 LEMON, CUT INTO WEDGES

08

PREPARATION

To make the koftas, mix together all the kofta ingredients until well blended. Divide into 10 -12 balls, then roll each ball on a board with a cupped hand to turn them into ovals.

Thread onto skewers and brush with oil. Heat the griddle pan until you can feel the heat rising and cook for 3-4 mins each side. Do not turn until they are well sealed, or the meat will stick to the grill.

Harissa salsa:

To make the harissa salsa, heat 1 tbsp oil in a pan over medium heat. Add onions, garlic and tomatoes, cook until fragrant. Add tomato puree and harissa spices. Season to taste.

Add mint leaves and lemon juice, mix well. Remove from the heat. Serve with lamb koftas.

LAMB KOFTAS AND WARM HARISSA SALSA

PREP TIME
15 MINS

COOKING TIME
20 MINS

SERVING
3-4 PERSONS

DIFFICULTY
○ ☑ ○ ○ ○

INGREDIENTS

KOFTAS:
500G LAMB MINCE
1 TSP GROUND CUMIN
2 TSP GROUND CORIANDER
2 GARLIC CLOVES, CRUSHED
1 TBSP CHOPPED MINT
SALT AND PAPER
2 TBSP OIL
12 BAMBOO SKEWERS

HARISSA SALSA:
2 TOMATOES, CHOPPED
1 SMALL ONION, CHOPPED
1 GARLIC, CRUSHED
1 TSP TOMATO PUREE
1 TSP CHOPPED MINT LEAVES
1/4 LEMON JUICE
1 TSP HARISSA SPICES
SALT AND PEPPER

09

PREPARATION

Put the eggs into a pan of boiling water, ensure that the eggs are covered in water. Cook for 6 minutes then rinse them in ice-cold water. Peel carefully. Set aside.

To make the masala mayonnaise, mix the mayonnaise with the garam masala and lemon juice in a bowl. Put aside.

In a bowl, mix the turkey mince, onion, garlic, garam masala, coriander, cumin, chilli flakes and chopped coriander leaves. Season with salt and paper. Set aside.

Mix two eggs in a bowl. Prepare the flour and breadcrumbs in two separate bowls.

Take one boiled egg and dust with the flour.

Cover the egg with the minced turkey, coat it with the flour, dip it in the egg mixture and coat it in the breadcrumbs. Repeat the process for all the eggs and put aside.

In a frying pan, heat up enough oil for frying the eggs over medium heat.

Fry the eggs until golden brown, approximately for 5 minutes. Keep basting the eggs with the oil, to ensure they are evenly fried. Remove from the frying pan and transfer to a plate. Serve with masala mayonnaise.

TURKEY SCOTCH EGGS WITH MASALA MAYONNAISE

PREP TIME
20 MINS

COOKING TIME
20 MINS

SERVING
6 PERSONS

DIFFICULTY
○ ○ ☑ ○ ○

INGREDIENTS

6 EGGS, SOFT BOILED
TURKEY MINCE:
450G TURKEY MINCE
2 GARLIC CLOVES, FINELY MINCED
1 MEDIUM ONION
A SMALL HANDFUL OF
CORIANDER LEAVES
1 TSP GARAM MASALA
1 TSP GROUND CORIANDER
½ TSP GROUND CUMIN

½ TSP CHILLI FLAKES
(ACCORDING TO TASTE)
SALT AND PEPPER

COATING:
3 TBSP PLAIN FLOUR
200G PANKO BREADCRUMBS
2 EGGS FOR COATING
FRYING OIL

10

PORK, CABBAGE AND CHIVE GYOZA

PREP TIME
1 HOUR

COOKING TIME
30 MINS

SERVING
10 PERSONS

DIFFICULTY
○ ○ ✓ ○ ○

INGREDIENTS

GYOZA:
500G CHINESE CABBAGE, SLICED THINLY
2 TSP SALT
500G MINCED PORK
2CM GINGER, MINCED
4 SPRING ONIONS, CHOPPED
3 GARLIC CLOVES, MINCED
2 TBSP SUGAR
SALT AND PEPPER
30 - 40 GYOZA/DUMPLING WRAPPERS
COOKING OIL

SAUCE:
120ML RICE VINEGAR
30ML LIGHT SOY SAUCE
2 TBSP CHILLI OIL (OPTIONAL)

PREPARATION

In a bowl, mix cabbage and 2 tsp of salt and leave the mixture for 15 mins. Transfer the cabbage into a clean tea towel. Squeeze out the liquid as much as possible.
In a large bowl, mix the drained cabbage, pork mince, ginger, spring onions, garlic, sugar, salt and pepper. Knead well with hand until the mixture feels sticky.
Take a small amount of filling and put it in the centre of the wrapper. Dip one finger in a bowl of water and draw a circle around the edge of the wrapper. Fold the wrapper in half over the filling and pinch it in the centre. Pleat the top part of the wrapper from the centre toward the right. As you fold each pleat, press the folded pleat tightly against the back part of wrapper. Once you make 3-4 pleats, pleat the left side of the gyoza from the centre to the left.

The dumplings can be frozen up to 2 months. To freeze, place dumplings on a baking sheet, freeze for 30 mins, and transfer to a freezer bag. Dumplings can be cooked directly from frozen.

Heat 1 tbsp of oil in a non-stick skillet over medium heat until shimmering. Add as many dumplings as will fit in a single layer and cook, until evenly golden brown on the bottom surface (about 1.5 minutes). Increase heat to medium-high, add 100-120ml water and cover tightly with a lid. Let dumplings steam for 3 minutes (5 minutes if frozen), then remove the lid. Continue cooking, swirl the pan frequently and use a thin spatula to gently dislodge the dumplings if they are stuck to the bottom of the pan, until the water has fully evaporated and the dumplings have crisped again (about 2 mins longer). Transfer to a plate. To make the sauce, mix the vinegar, soy and chilli oil.

11 | KALE, QUINOA, COUSCOUS AND ROAST CHICKEN SALAD

DIFFICULTY	PREP TIME	COOKING TIME	SERVING
⊘○○○○	10 MINS	30 MINS	2 PERSONS

INGREDIENTS

2 CHICKEN FILLETS

2 TBSP OLIVE OIL

1 LEMON JUICE

2 TSP HARISSA SPICE

2 HANDFULS OF KALE

100G COOKED QUINOA

100G COOKED COUSCOUS

1/2 TSP CHILLI POWDER

SALT AND PEPPER

PREPARATION

Turn on the oven to 200C/gas 6.

Put the chicken fillets on a baking tray, drizzle with 1 tbsp olive oil, 1/2 lemon juice, 1 tsp harissa spice, salt and pepper. Roast for 20 mins or until cooked.

Put the kale in a bowl, add 1 tbsp of olive oil, squeeze and massage the kale until soft.

Add cooked quinoa and couscous, 1 tsp harissa powder, chilli powder, lemon juice and salt and pepper, into the bowl. Mix well and taste. Season to taste. Transfer into plates.

Take out the roast chicken fillets, slice and serve them on top of the salad.

12 | SUPER PINK SALAD

DIFFICULTY
⊘ ○ ○ ○ ○

PREP TIME
10 MINS

SERVING
2 PERSONS

INGREDIENTS

1 TBSP OLIVE OIL

1 LEMON JUICE

100G COOKED QUINOA

100G COOKED COUSCOUS

4 TBSP SOYBEANS

4 TBSP SWEETCORN

2 BEETROOTS, CUT INTO CHUNKS

2-3 ICEBERG/ROMANO LETTUCE
LEAVES, SLICED

PREPARATION

In a small bowl, mix the olive oil and lemon juice. In a large bowl mix the quinoa, couscous, soybeans, sweetcorn, pomegranate, beetroot and lettuce.
Drizzle the salad with the olive oil and lemon juice mixture. Mix well and serve.

SEA FOOD

13

BASA FILLETS IN HERBY LEMON BUTTER SAUCE

PREP TIME
5 MINS

COOKING TIME
10 MINS

SERVING
2 PERSONS

DIFFICULTY
○ ✓ ○ ○ ○

INGREDIENTS

3 TBSP BUTTER
1 GARLIC CLOVE, FINELY MINCED
2 BASA FILLETS
1 TBSP ITALIAN HERBS
A SMALL BUNCH OF PARSLEY,
CHOPPED
1/2 LEMON JUICE
SALT AND PEPPER

PREPARATION

Melt the butter in a skillet over medium heat. Add the minced garlic, cook for 1 minute until fragrant. Add the Italian herbs, cook for another 2 minutes.
Add the basa fillets, baste with the sauce to add more flavour.
Cook until the fillets are tender for about 4-5 mins.
Season to taste.
Add the lemon juice and fresh parsley.
Cook for another minute, remove from the heat and serve.

14

HADDOCK PIE

PREP TIME
15 MINS

COOKING TIME
45 MINS

SERVING
4 PERSONS

DIFFICULTY
○ ○ ⊘ ○ ○

INGREDIENTS

1KG POTATOES, PEELED, QUARTERED
400ML MILK, PLUS 2 TBSP
A PINCH OF BLACK PEPPER
3 TBSP BUTTER
3 TBSP PLAIN FLOUR
1 ONION, CHOPPED
200G HADDOCK FILLETS
200G SMOKED HADDOCK FILLETS
1 TSP DIJON OR ENGLISH MUSTARD
A SMALL BUNCH OF PARSLEY, FINELY CHOPPED
100G FROZEN PEAS
A HANDFUL GRATED CHEDDAR

PREPARATION

Pre-heat the oven to 200C/gas mark 6. Boil the potatoes in a large pan and then simmer until cooked and soft. Drain the potatoes and mash with 2 tbsp milk and 1 tbsp butter. Season with the black pepper. Melt the butter in another large pan and sauté the onion until soft. Stir in the flour and cook for 3 mins. Gradually whisk in the milk. Bring to the boil, stirring to avoid any lumps and sticking at the bottom of the pan. Cook for 3 – 4 minutes until thickened. Take off the heat and stir in the haddock and smoked haddock, 1 tsp Dijon mustard, parsley and peas. Transfer into a pie dish. Spread the mashed potato on top and sprinkle with the grated cheddar cheese. At this point, the pie can be frozen for another time.
Bake the pie in the oven for 20 - 25 mins or until golden and bubbling at the edges.

31

15

PAN FRIED SEABASS WITH SPRING ONION, GINGER, CHILLI AND GARLIC

PREP TIME
15 MINS

COOKING TIME
10 MINS

SERVING
2 PERSONS

DIFFICULTY
○ ☑ ○ ○ ○

INGREDIENTS

2 SEA BASS FILLETS, SKIN ON AND SCALED
SALT AND PEPPER
2 TBSP COOKING OIL
2CM GINGER, PEELED AND JULIENNED
2 GARLIC CLOVES, THINLY SLICED
1 LARGE RED CHILLI, DESEEDED AND JULIENNED
2 BIRD EYE CHILLIES, THINLY SLICED
5 BUNCH SPRING ONION, JULIENNED
2 TBSP LIGHT SOY SAUCE
1 TBSP SESAME OIL
1 TBSP SHAOXING RICE WINE

PREPARATION

Season the fish with salt and pepper, then slash the skin 3 times.

Heat a frying pan and add 1 tbsp oil. Once hot, fry the fish, skin-side down, for 5 mins or until the skin is very crisp and golden. Turn over, cook for another 30 secs–1 min. Transfer to a serving plate and keep warm.

Heat the remaining oil together with sesame oil. Add ginger, garlic and chillies for about 1 min. Add soy sauce and Shaoxing rice wine. Cook until the sauce bubbles. Season to taste. Take off the heat and toss in the spring onions. Serve the sauce on top of the fish.

16

PAN FRIED TROUT IN SWEET AND SPICY SHALLOT SAUCE

PREP TIME
15 MINS

COOKING TIME
20 MINS

SERVING
2 PERSONS

DIFFICULTY
○ ✓ ○ ○ ○

INGREDIENTS

2 TROUT FILLETS
A PINCH OF SALT
1 LIME JUICE
3 TBSP COOKING OIL
5 SHALLOTS, THINLY SLICED
2 GARLIC CLOVES, FINELY MINCED
2 GREEN AND RED CHILLIES, SLICED
1 TOMATO, ROUGHLY CHOPPED
1CM GALANGAL, CRUSHED
1/3 OF LEMON GRASS, CRUSHED
2 LIME LEAVES
5-6 TBSP KECAP MANIS
SALT AND PEPPER

PREPARATION

Season the fish with a pinch of salt and ½ lime juice. Heat the oil in a frying pan over medium heat. Fry the fish fillets for 4 minutes each side, skin first. Once cooked, remove from the heat and put them on a serving dish. Remove excess oil from the frying pan. In the same pan, sauté the shallots, garlic, chillies, tomato, galangal, lemongrass and lime leaves for 4-5 minutes until fragrant and the shallots are soft. Add the kecap manis and lime juice. Cook until the sauce bubbles. Season to taste with salt and pepper. Stir one more time and turn off the heat. Pour the sauce over the pan-fried fish fillets and serve with steamed rice.

17

PREPARATION

In a food processor blend all of the sauce ingredients until smooth. Season to taste. In a large bowl mix the sauce with the tuna cubes, chopped tomatoes and basil leaves. Put together two sheets of banana leaves (approx. 20cm x 20cm) place 1 bay leave on top of the leaves followed by 3-4 tbsp of tuna mixture in the middle of the sheets. Roll the banana leaves to wrap the tuna and secure with toothpicks in each end. Repeat the process until the tuna are finished.

Prepare a steamer. When it is ready, steam the wrapped tuna for 30 minutes. Remove from the steamer and let them dry.

Heat up a griddle pan over medium heat, add 1 tbsp of oil. Grill the wrapped tuna for 3-4 mins until all sides are turning brown. Turn off the heat and serve the tuna with steamed rice.

AROMATIC TUNA WRAPPED IN BANANA LEAF (PEPES IKAN TUNA)

PREP TIME
15 MINS

COOKING TIME
45 MINS

SERVING
6 PERSONS

DIFFICULTY
○ ☑ ○ ○ ○

INGREDIENTS

800G TUNA STEAKS, CUBED
4 TOMATOES, ROUGHLY CHOPPED
50G (HOLY) BASIL LEAVES BANANA
LEAVES AND TOOTHPICKS TO WRAP
4 BAY LEAVES
1 TBSP COOKING OIL FOR GRILLING

SAUCE
5 LARGE RED CHILLIES, CUT INTO
LARGE PIECES
3-5 BIRD EYE CHILLIES
2 SLICES GALANGAL, ROUGHLY
CHOPPED
2 LEMONGRASS, ROUGHLY CHOPPED
1 SLICE GINGER

6 LIME LEAVES
4 GARLIC CLOVES
6 SHALLOTS
4 CANDLENUTS, SLIGHTLY ROASTED
1 TSP GROUND TURMERIC
½ TBSP COOKING OIL
SALT PEPPER

18

SMOKED MACKEREL CURRY

PREP TIME
5 MINS

COOKING TIME
15 MINS

SERVING
2-3 PERSONS

DIFFICULTY
○ ☑ ○ ○ ○

INGREDIENTS

1 TBSP COOKING OIL
1 GREEN PEPPER, DESEEDED AND
ROUGHLY CHOPPED
2 GARLIC CLOVES, FINELY MINCED
2 SHALLOTS, FINELY CHOPPED
½ TBSP CRUSHED CHILLIES
¼- ½ TBSP GROUND TURMERIC
3 LIME LEAVES
1 LEMONGRASS, CRUSHED THE WHITE
PART AND DIVIDED INTO THREE
2 SLICES OF GALANGAL
200G SMOKED MACKEREL FILLET, CUT
EACH FILLET INTO TWO.
1 TIN OF COCONUT MILK
1/2 – 1 LEMON JUICE
SALT AND PEPPER
A SMALL BUNCH OF CORIANDER
LEAVES, CHOPPED

PREPARATION

In a wok or large saucepan, sauté the green pepper, garlic, shallots, chillies, turmeric, lime leaves, lemongrass and galangal for 2-3 minutes. When the shallots are soft add the coconut milk and bring to boil. Add the smoked mackerel. Cook for 2-3 minutes. Stir in the lemon juice and season to taste. Turn off the heat and garnish with coriander leaves. Serve the curry with steamed rice.

19

THAI AROMATIC STEAMED MUSSELS

PREP TIME
10 MINS

COOKING TIME
15 MINS

SERVING
4-6 PERSONS

DIFFICULTY
○ ☑ ○ ○ ○

INGREDIENTS

3 SHALLOTS, MINCED
2 GARLIC CLOVES, MINCED
1 LEMONGRASS, CUT INTO THREE
PIECES, CRUSHED
2CM GALANGAL, CRUSHED
2CM GINGER, SLICED
1-2 RED AND GREEN CHILLIES
(ACCORDING TO TASTE)
1/2 LEMON JUICE AND ZEST
SALT AND PEPPER
1KG MUSSELS
750ML CHICKEN STOCK
2 TBSP SHAOXING RED WINE
1 SMALL HANDFUL CORIANDER
LEAVES, CHOPPED

PREPARATION

Sauté shallots, garlic, lemongrass, galangal, ginger, chillies and lemon zest in a large pot with a lid, over medium heat. Cook until aromatic and shallots are soft. Add a pinch of salt and pepper. Add mussels and give a good toss. Add Shaoxing rice wine, lemon juice and chicken stocks. Cover the pot and steam over medium-high for 5 minutes until the mussels open. Season to taste, garnish with chopped coriander leaves and serve.

20

SALT AND PEPPER SQUIDS

PREP TIME
20 MINS

COOKING TIME
20 MINS

SERVING
4 PERSONS

DIFFICULTY
○ ☑ ○ ○ ○

INGREDIENTS

500G SQUID TUBES
1 EGG
200G CORNFLOUR
COOKING OIL FOR FRYING PLUS
1 TBSP
½ TBSP SESAME OIL
2 GARLIC CLOVES, FINELY MINCED
1 BIG RED CHILLI, THINLY SLICED
2 BIRD EYE CHILLIES, CHOPPED
3 SPRING ONIONS, CHOPPED
1 TSP CHINESE FIVE-SPICE

PREPARATION

Cut each squid hood in half lengthways. Using a sharp knife score inside in a criss-cross pattern. Cut each piece in half lengthways. Cut each strip crossways into 4 pieces. Pat dry with a paper towel.

In a large bowl mix the egg with 1 tbsp cornflour. Add pinches of salt, pepper and garlic powder. Add the squids and mix well.

In another bowl shift the rest of the cornflour, and pinches of salt, pepper and garlic powder. In a big frying pan heat the oil over medium heat.

Add the squid pieces into the flour mix, cover each piece with flour and remove excess flour. If necessary, make another batch of egg and flour mixes.

Fry the squid pieces until golden brown, remove and transfer to a plate covered with a kitchen towel. Do not overcook and you may want to cook them in batches.

In a wok, drizzle 1 tbsp cooking oil and sesame oil over medium-high heat. Add minced garlic, spring onions, and chillies. Season with salt, pepper and Chinese five spices. Add fried squids and mix well. Transfer to a plate.

21

MALAYSIAN BUTTER PRAWNS

PREP TIME
20 MINS

COOKING TIME
30 MINS

SERVING
2 PERSONS

DIFFICULTY
○ ○ ✓ ○ ○

INGREDIENTS

8-10 TIGER PRAWNS, REMOVE
HEADS AND VEIN AND KEEP SHELLS
AND TAILS ON
4 TBSP CORNFLOUR
COOKING OIL FOR FRYING PLUS
1 TBSP
100G DESICCATED COCONUT
1-2 TBSP BUTTER
6 SHALLOTS, CHOPPED
3 GARLIC CLOVES, FINELY MINCED
2 LARGE RED AND GREEN CHILLIES
2 BIRD EYE CHILLIES (ACCORDING
TO TASTE)
8 CURRY LEAVES
½ TBSP SHAOXING RICE WINE
SALT AND PAPER

PREPARATION

Pat the prawns dry using paper towels.
Cover the prawns in cornflour, remove
excess flour. Deep the prawns until
golden brown and set aside. Meanwhile,
toast the desiccated coconut in a non-
stick frying pan until golden. Remove from
the heat and set aside. Melt the butter in
a wok over medium-high heat. Sauté the
shallots, garlic, chillies, curry leaves and
Shaoxing rice wine until fragrant. Stir in
the desiccated coconut. Season to taste
with salt and pepper. Add the prawns into
the wok and mix well. Turn off the heat
and serve the prawns with steamed rice.

22

STIR FRIED PRAWNS WITH BABY CORN AND RUNNER BEANS IN OYSTER SAUCE

PREP TIME
5 MINS

COOKING TIME
10 MINS

SERVING
2-3 PERSONS

DIFFICULTY
○ ☑ ○ ○ ○

INGREDIENTS

1 TBSP COOKING OIL

2 GARLIC CLOVES, FINELY MINCED

1CM GINGER, CRUSHED

1 TSP CHILLI FLAKES

125G BABY CORN, SLICED

125G RUNNER BEANS, SLICED

250G PEELED PRAWNS

1 TBSP SESAME OIL

2-3 TBSP SOY SAUCE

3-4 TBSP OYSTER SAUCE

1 TBSP SHAOXING RICE WINE

SALT AND PEPPER

PREPARATION

Heat the cooking oil in a wok. Sauté the garlic, ginger and chilli for 30 seconds until fragrant but not burnt. Add the baby corn and runner beans. Cook until the vegetables are almost soft. Add the prawns, cook for 5 mins until they are cooked. Season to taste with sesame oil, soy sauce, oyster sauce, Shaoxing rice wine, salt and pepper. Stir one more time, turn off the heat and serve with steamed rice.

CHICKEN

23

PREPARATION

In a large bowl mix the yoghurt, garlic, lemon juice, tomato puree, coriander, cumin, turmeric, paprika, chilli and black pepper. Season to taste. Mix in the chicken fillets. Refrigerate for 1 hr or overnight.

Thread the chicken pieces, pepper, onion, mushroom and courgette onto metal or bamboo skewers.

Grill the chicken skewers on a BBQ grill or a griddle pan. If using griddle pan, spray the pan with some cooking oil. Grill until the chicken is cooked. 3-4 mins each side. Garnish the kebab with chopped coriander leaves.

To make the cucumber raita, mix all ingredients into a bowl and refrigerate before serving.

Serve the kebab and raita with tortilla wraps, flatbread or rice.

CHICKEN KEBAB

PREP TIME
10 MINS

COOKING TIME
20 MINS

SERVING
2 PERSONS

DIFFICULTY
○ ⊘ ○ ○ ○

INGREDIENTS

300G GREEK YOGHURT
2 GARLIC CLOVES, MINCED
½ LEMON JUICE
1 TBSP TOMATO PUREE
2 TSP GROUND CORIANDER
1 TSP GROUND CUMIN
1 TSP GROUND TURMERIC
1 TSP PAPRIKA
½ - 1 TSP CHILLI POWDER
1 TSP BLACK PEPPER
500G CHICKEN THIGH FILLETS, CUT
INTO PIECES
1 SMALL ONION, PEELED, QUARTERED
AND LAYERS SEPARATED
1 PEPPER

6-8 BUTTON MUSHROOMS
½ COURGETTE, CUT INTO CHUNKS

CUCUMBER RAITA
200G GREEK YOGHURT
1 CUCUMBER, PEELED, DESEEDED
AND CHOPPED
1 TBSP CHOPPED MINT AND
CORIANDER LEAVES
1 GARLIC CLOVE, FINELY MINCED
¼ TSP CHILLI OR PAPRIKA POWDER

51

24

TUMERIC FRIED CHICKEN
(AYAM GORENG KUNYIT)

PREP TIME
10 MINS

COOKING TIME
30 MINS

SERVING
4 PERSONS

DIFFICULTY
○ ○ ✓ ○ ○

INGREDIENTS

2 EGGS
100G CORNFLOUR
SALT AND PEPPER
500G BONELESS CHICKEN THIGHS, CUT INTO LARGE CHUNKS
5 SHALLOTS, CHOPPED
3 GARLIC, MINCED
3-4 LARGE RED AND GREEN CHILLIES, SLICED
2 BIRD EYE CHILLIES, SLICED
1 LEMONGRASS, CRUSH THE WHITE PART AND CUT INTO 2-3 PARTS
2CM GALANGAL, SLICED
6 LIME LEAVES
1 TBSP TURMERIC
½ TBSP GROUND CORIANDER
¼ - ½ TBSP GROUND CUMIN
COOKING OIL

PREPARATION

In a bowl beat the eggs with 1/2 tbsp of cornflour and sprinkles of salt and pepper. Add the chicken and mix well. Heat up the oil in a wok for frying. Generously coat each chicken chunk with the cornflour. Deep fry the chicken until cooked and golden. Set aside.

In a large wok, sauté the shallots, garlic, chillies, galangal, lime leaves until the shallots are soft. Season to taste with turmeric, coriander, cumin, salt and pepper. Stir in the fried chicken and ensure that they are coated with the spices. Turn off the heat and serve with steamed rice.

25

CHICKEN CACCIATORE

PREP TIME
10 MINS

COOKING TIME
25 MINS

SERVING
6-8 PERSONS

DIFFICULTY

○ ○ ⊘ ○ ○

INGREDIENTS

8 CHICKEN THIGH/BREAST FILLETS
3 TBSP OLIVE OIL
50G ANCHOVIES IN OLIVE OIL
2 ONIONS, CHOPPED
3 GARLIC, MINCED
3 TOMATOES, CHOPPED
200ML WHITE WINE
1 RED PEPPER, SLICED
1 YELLOW PEPPER, SLICED
1 TIN OF PLUM TOMATOES
500G PASSATA
1 TBSP TOMATO PUREE
1-2 TBSP DRIED ITALIAN HERBS
340G PITTED BLACK OLIVES IN A
JAR, DRAINED
1 SMALL HANDFUL OF BASIL
LEAVES, ROUGHLY CHOPPED

PREPARATION

In a large frying pan, brown the chicken fillets, 2 mins on each side. Remove the chicken from the pan and set aside. In the same pan, sauté the anchovies, onion, garlic and tomatoes. Add the white wine and let the wine reduced slightly. Add red and yellow peppers and stir. Add the plum tomatoes, passata, tomato puree and Italian herbs. Let the sauce bubbles and simmer for 10-15 mins. Season to taste. Add the chicken fillets into the sauce mixture and let them cook through. Add the black olives and stir. Turn off the heat, transfer to a serving dish and garnish with the basil leaves.

26

HONEY SRIRACHA CHICKEN WINGS

PREP TIME
10 MINS

COOKING TIME
55 MINS

SERVING
4 PERSONS

DIFFICULTY
○ ⊘ ○ ○ ○

INGREDIENTS

2 TBSP BAKING POWDER
1 TBSP SALT
1 TSP PEPPER
1 TSP SMOKED PAPRIKA
1KG CHICKEN WINGS
1-2 TSP TOASTED SESAME SEEDS
1 SMALL HANDFUL CORIANDER
LEAVES, CHOPPED

HONEY SRIRACHA GLAZE:
6 TBSP HONEY
6 TBSP SRIRACHA SAUCE
1 TBSP SHAOXING RICE WINE
1 TBSP SESAME OIL

PREPARATION

Pre-heat oven to 220C/gas mark 7. Mix the baking powder, salt, pepper and smoked paprika in a large bowl. Add the chicken wings into the bowl. Coat the wings with the spice mixture. Place the wings in a baking sheet lined with aluminium foil. Place chicken wings in a large bowl. Bake for 20 mins. Turn the wings and bake for another 20 mins. Turn the wings again, bake for 15 mins until brown and crispy.
In a bowl, mix all glazing ingredients until smooth. Coat the wings with the glaze. Transfer to a serving plate and sprinkle with toasted sesame seeds and chopped coriander.

27

SLOW COOK ASIAN SWEET AND SPICY CHICKEN DRUMSTICKS

PREP TIME
5 MINS

COOKING TIME
4 (HIGH) OR 6 HRS (LOW)

SERVING
5 PERSONS

DIFFICULTY
✓ ○ ○ ○ ○

INGREDIENTS

750G CHICKEN DRUMSTICKS

MARINADE:
6 TBSP SWEET CHILLI SAUCE
3-4 TBSP SOY SAUCE
1 TBSP SHAOXING RICE WINE
1 TBSP SESAME OIL
1 TBSP MINCED GARLIC
1 LEMONGRASS, CRUSH THE WHITE PART AND CUT INTO THREE
2CM GALANGAL, CRUSHED
2CM GINGER, CRUSHED

PREPARATION

Mix all marinating ingredients in the slow cooker. Season to taste. Add the chicken drumsticks, mix well. Slow cook for 4 hours (high) or 6 hours (low). Stir occasionally. Serve with steam rice.

28

SLOW COOKED PULLED CHICKEN TACOS

PREP TIME	COOKING TIME	SERVING
10 MINS	4-5 HOURS (SLOW) OR 3 HOURS (HIGH)	4 PERSONS

DIFFICULTY

INGREDIENTS

1KG CHICKEN BREAST

1 LARGE ONION, FINELY CHOPPED

60G FAJITA SEASONING

1 TSP CHILLI FLAKES

1 TSP PAPRIKA

12 TACO SHELLS

SALT AND PEPPER

PREPARATION

In a slow cooker, mix chicken breasts, onion, fajita seasoning, chilli flakes, paprika and pinches of salt and pepper.
Slow cook for 4-5 hours (slow) or 3 hours (high).
One hour before finish cooking, season to taste.
Once the chicken is tender, shred using two forks.
Fill in taco shells with chicken and serve with a simple salad.

29

CAJUN SPICED CHICKEN AND KIDNEY BEANS

PREP TIME
5 MINS

MARINATE
30 MINS

COOKING TIME
15 MINS

SERVING
3 PERSONS

DIFFICULTY
○ ☑ ○ ○ ○

INGREDIENTS

500G CHICKEN FILLETS, CUBED
1-2 TBSP CAJUN SEASONING
1 TBSP OLIVE OIL
1 ONION, CHOPPED
2 GARLIC CLOVES, MINCED
1 TIN OF TOMATOES
1 PEPPER, CHOPPED
1 TSP CHILLI FLAKES (ACCORDING
TO TASTE)
1 TIN KIDNEY BEANS
1 LEMON JUICE
1 HANDFUL OF CORIANDER
LEAVES, CHOPPED
SALT AND PEPPER

PREPARATION

Marinate the chicken with the Cajun seasoning for at least for half an hour. Sauté the onion and garlic in a large frying pan until fragrant. Add the marinated chicken and cook for 3 minutes. Add the tin of tomatoes, pepper and chilli flakes. Mix well and season to taste. Let the sauce bubble and the chicken is cooked. Stir in the kidney beans and lemon juice. Cook for another 2 mins. Remove from the heat. Garnish with coriander leaves. Turn off the heat and serve with tortilla wraps or tacos.

30

SPICY THAI BASIL TURKEY
(TURKEY PAD KRAPOW)

PREP TIME
10 MINS

COOKING TIME
15 MINS

SERVING
3-4 PERSONS

DIFFICULTY
○ ☑ ○ ○ ○

INGREDIENTS

1 TBSP COOKING OIL
1 LARGE RED ONION, FINELY MINCED
3 CLOVES OF GARLIC, FINELY MINCED
1/2 TBSP CRUSHED CHILLI OR BIRD-EYE CHILLI (ACCORDING TO TASTE)
1 LEMONGRASS, CRUSH THE WHITE, AND CHOP INTO 3 PARTS
2CM GALANGAL, CRUSHED
4-5 LIME LEAVES
400G MINCED TURKEY MEAT
2 MIXED PEPPERS, SLICED
1/2-1 TBSP FISH SAUCE
1/2 TBSP DARK SOY SAUCE
1 TBSP LIGHT SOY SAUCE
1 TBSP KECAP MANIS
1/2 TBSP BROWN SUGAR
SALT AND PEPPER
1 SMALL BUNCH (HOLY) BASIL

PREPARATION

In a wok, sauté the red onion, garlic, chilli, lemongrass, galangal and lime leaves until the onion is soft and fragrant. Add the minced meat, brown for 5-6 mins. Add the sliced peppers, mix well. Add the fish sauce, dark and light soy sauce, kecap manis, brown sugar and salt and pepper. Season to taste. Cook for another 3 mins. Add basil leaves. Mix well. Turn off the heat. Transfer to a plate and serve with a fried sunny egg and steamed rice.

31

BALINESE CHICKEN CURRY
(AYAM BALI)

PREP TIME
15 MINS

COOKING TIME
20 MINS

SERVING
4 PERSONS

DIFFICULTY
○ ☑ ○ ○ ○

INGREDIENTS

50G CHICKEN BREAST FILLET
1 TBSP COOKING OIL
1 LEMONGRASS, CRUSH THE WHITE PART AND CUT INTO 3 PARTS
2CM GALANGAL, CRUSHED
2CM GINGER, SLICED
4-5 LIME LEAVES
2 TBSP TOMATO PUREE
SALT AND PEPPER
1/2 LEMON JUICE
SAUCE:
1 LARGE RED ONION, QUARTERED
3 CLOVES OF GARLIC
3 TOMATOES, QUARTERED
6 LARGE RED CHILLIES, CUT INTO 4 PARTS
½ TBSP COOKING OIL

PREPARATION

In a food processor, blend the red onion, garlic, tomatoes, red chillies and ½ tbsp cooking oil. In a large wok, sauté the sauce mixture with 1 tbsp cooking oil. Add the lemongrass, galangal, ginger, lime leaves, tomato puree. Turn down the heat and keep stirring so the sauce doesn't stick to the wok. Let the sauce bubble. Add the chicken cubes. Mix well and stir occasionally for 7-8 mins until the chicken is cooked. Season to taste and add the lemon juice. Stir one more time. Remove from the heat and serve with steamed rice.

32

SURINAMESE CHICKEN CURRY
(SURINAAMSE KIP KERRIE)

PREP TIME
10 MINS

COOKING TIME
20 MINS

SERVING
4 PERSONS

DIFFICULTY
○ ☑ ○ ○ ○

INGREDIENTS

1 TBSP COOKING OIL
1 ONION, CHOPPED
3 GARLIC CLOVES, MINCED
500G CHICKEN FILLETS, CUBED
½ TSP TOMATO PUREE
2 TBSP GARAM MASALA
1 TSP GROUND CORIANDER
½ TSP GROUND CUMIN
1 TSP CHILLI FLAKES (ACCORDING
TO TASTE)
200G RUNNER GREENS, CUT
DIAGONALLY
SALT AND PEPPER

PREPARATION

Sauté the onion and garlic in a large wok until the onion is soft. Add the chicken and cook for 3 mins. Add the tomato puree, garam masala, ground coriander, ground cumin and chilli flakes. Coat the chicken with the seasoning. Stir in the runner beans. Add a ladle of water and let it simmer for 10 mins until the chicken is cooked and the beans are soft. Season to taste. Turn off the heat and serve with roti (chapatti) or steamed rice.

MEAT

33

CHILLI BEAN PORK AND CHINESE CHIVES

PREP TIME
10 MINS

COOKING TIME
10 MINS

SERVING
4 PERSONS

DIFFICULTY
○ ⊘ ○ ○ ○

INGREDIENTS

500G PORK FILLETS, CUBED
4 TBSP CHILLI BEAN SAUCE
1 TBSP CORNFLOUR
1 TBSP COOKING OIL
1 ONION, SLICED
2 GARLIC CLOVES, MINCED
1 TOMATO, SLICED
1 TBSP LIGHT SOY SAUCE
1 TBSP SHAOXING RED WINE
1 TBSP SESAME OIL
SALT AND PEPPER
1 HANDFUL CHINESE CHIVES, CUT
2CM LONG

PREPARATION

In a bowl, mix pork cubes, chilli bean sauce and cornflour. Mix well and leave it for 1 hour or overnight. Sauté the onion, garlic and tomato in a wok over medium high heat until fragrant.
Stir in the light soy sauce, sesame oil and Shaoxing rice wine. Add the marinated pork. Keep stirring and add a bit of water to ensure the pork does not stick to the wok. Cook for 10 minutes or until the pork is cooked. Season to taste. Add the chives, stir well and cook for 1 min. Remove from the heat and transfer to a plate.

34

VIETNAMESE CARAMEL PORK

PREP TIME
5 MINS

COOKING TIME
1 HR 45 MINS

SERVING
4-5 PERSONS

DIFFICULTY
○ ☑ ○ ○ ○

INGREDIENTS

8 TBSP BROWN SUGAR
1KG PORK BELLY OR PORK
STEAKS WITH FAT, CUT INTO
CHUNKS
300ML COCONUT WATER
3 GARLIC CLOVES
2CM GINGER, CRUSHED
4 TSP FISH SAUCE
2 TBSP DARK SOY SAUCE
SALT AND PEPPER
1 LARGE RED CHILLI, DESEEDED
AND JULIENNED
1-2 SPRING ONIONS, JULIENNED

PREPARATION

In a large non-stick saucepan, dissolve that brown sugar and 1 tbsp water over high heat. Meanwhile, place the brown sugar and 1 tbsp water in a large saucepan over high heat. Cook for 4-5 minutes until the sugar dissolves and forms dark caramel. Add the pork to the pan and coat it with the caramel. Add the coconut water and bring to boil. Remove any impurities that rise to the surface. Add the garlic, ginger, fish sauce and dark soy sauce. Season with salt and pepper. Reduce the heat to low and simmer, uncovered, for 1 1/2 hours, until the pork is tender and the sauce is thick and glossy. Coat the pork with sauce. Season one more time and remove from the heat. Garnish with the julienned chilli and spring onions.

35

SLOW COOKED CHINESE STICKY PORK BELLY

PREP TIME
5 MINS

MARINATE
1HR OR OVERNIGHT

COOKING TIME
6HRS (LOW) 4 HRS (HIGH)

DIFFICULTY
○ ⊘ ○ ○ ○

INGREDIENTS

18 TBSP BROWN SUGAR
15 TBSP LIGHT SOY SAUCE
5 TBSP DARK SOY SAUCE
3 TBSP CHINESE FIVE-SPICE
5 TBSP CORNFLOUR
3 TBSP SESAME OIL
3 TBSP SHAOXING RICE WINE
SALT AND PEPPER
1.5KG PORK BELLY, CUBED
2CM×2CM×2CM
250G WHITE/CHESTNUT
MUSHROOMS, SLICED
2 TBSP COOKING OIL
2 WHITE ONIONS, SLICED
4 GARLIC CLOVES, FINELY CHOPPED

PREPARATION

In a bowl, mix the brown sugar, light and dark soy sauce, Chinese five-spice, cornflour, sesame oil, Shaoxing rice wine, salt and pepper. Season to taste.
Add the pork belly cubes. Mix well. Leave to marinate for at least one hour or overnight.
Heat the cooking oil in a wok or big frying pan, add the onions and garlic, cook until soft and fragrant.
Add the pork marinated pork belly and mushrooms, cook for 10 mins, mix well with the onions and garlic.
Transfer to a slow cooker. Cook for 6hrs (low) or 4hrs (high). Season to taste.
Once cooked, serve with steamed rice and stir-fried vegetables.

36

PREPARATION

To make the deep fried pork balls, heat the frying oil in a large wok over medium-high heat. In a bowl, lightly beat the egg with 1 tsp cornflour. Put the rest of the cornflour in another bowl, season with a pinch of salt and pepper. Dip the pork chunks into the egg mixture and coat them with seasoned cornflour. Remove any excess flour, and deep fry the pork until they are cooked and golden. Remove from the wok and put aside. You may have to do this in two batches.

To make the sweet and sour sauce, mix the ketchup, pineapple syrup, soy sauce, oyster sauce, sugar, sesame oil and Shaoxing rice wine in a bowl.

Heat the cooking oil in a wok over medium-high heat. Add the spring onion whites, onion, garlic and ginger slices. Cook until fragrant. Add the red and green peppers. Cook for 2-3 mins until the onion and peppers are tender. Add the sauce mixture. Mix well, let the sauce bubbles and season to taste. Stir in the diluted cornflour, mix well. If the sauce is too thick, add some water. Add the pork and pineapple. Mix everything well. Cook for another 1-2 mins. Season to taste one more time. Turn of the heat. Serve the sweet and sour pork with steamed rice and stir-fried vegetables.

SWEET AND SOUR PORK

PREP TIME
15 MINS

COOKING TIME
30 MINS

SERVING
3-4 PERSONS

DIFFICULTY

INGREDIENTS

½ TBSP COOKING OIL
½ RED PEPPER
½ GREEN PEPPER
217G PINEAPPLE CHUNKS IN SYRUP,
DRAIN AND KEEP THE SYRUP
2 GARLIC MINCED
4 SPRING ONIONS, CUT INTO 5-6
PARTS, SEPARATE THE WHITES AND
GREEN PARTS
1 ONION, QUARTERED

DEEP FRIED PORK BALLS
OIL FOR FRYING
4 PORK STEAKS, CUBED
1 EGG, LIGHTLY BEATEN

8-10 TBSP CORNFLOUR
SALT AND PEPPER
½ TBSP CORNFLOUR, DILUTED WITH
3 TBSP WATER

SWEET AND SOUR SAUCE
5-6 TBSP TOMATO KETCHUP
SYRUP FROM THE PINEAPPLE
CHUNKS
1 TBSP SOY SAUCE
1 TBSP OYSTER SAUCE
½ - 1 TBSP SUGAR
1 TBSP SESAME OIL
1 TBSP SHAOXING RED WINE

37

SWEDISH MEATBALLS

PREP TIME
15 MINS

COOKING TIME
20 MINS

SERVING
4 PERSONS

DIFFICULTY
○ ☑ ○ ○ ○

INGREDIENTS

400G PORK MINCE
1 EGG, BEATEN
1 WHITE ONION, FINELY CHOPPED
85G BREADCRUMBS
2 TBSP OLIVE OIL
1 TBSP BUTTER
2 TBSP PLAIN FLOUR
400ML HOT PORK STOCK
A PINCH OF NUTMEG
A PINCH OF CINNAMON
SALT AND PEPPER TO SEASON
2 TBSP PARSLEY, FINELY CHOPPED

PREPARATION

Mix the mince with the egg, onion, breadcrumbs, salt and pepper and form into small meatballs.

Heat the olive oil in a large non-stick frying pan and brown the meatballs.

Remove the meatballs from the pan, melt the butter, then sprinkle over the flour and stir well. Cook for 2 mins, then slowly whisk in the stock.

Keep whisking until it is a thick gravy, then return the meatballs to the pan and heat through. Season to taste with nutmeg, cinnamon, salt and pepper. Turn off the heat and garnish with the chopped parsley.

Serve the meatballs with mashed potato or pasta.

38

COCONUT LAMB CURRY

PREP TIME
10 MINS

COOKING TIME
30 MINS

SERVING
3-4 PERSONS

DIFFICULTY
○ ✓ ○ ○ ○

INGREDIENTS

1 TBSP COOKING OIL
1 ONION, FINELY DICED
3 GARLIC CLOVES, FINELY DICED
5 BIG GREEN CHILLIES, SLICED
3 LIME LEAVES
400G LAMB FILLET, CUBED
1 TBSP CURRY POWDER
1/2 TBSP GROUND CORIANDER
1/2 TBSP GROUND TURMERIC
1 TSP GROUND CUMIN
1 TIN OF COCONUT MILK
SALT AND PEPPER
1/2 LEMON JUICE
A SMALL BUNCH OF CORIANDER
LEAVES, CHOPPED

PREPARATION

Heat the oil in a wok or frying pan over medium heat. Add the onion, garlic, chillies, lime leaves, cook until fragrant and the onion is soft. Add the lamb fillets, curry powder, coriander, turmeric and cumin. Mix until the fillets are coated with spices. Cook for 5 minutes. Add the coconut milk, stir occasionally and let it boil. Season to taste and lower the heat. Cook until the lamb is soft and tender (10-15 mins). Add the lemon juice, stir. Remove from the heat. Transfer to a bowl and garnish with the coriander leaves. Serve the curry with naan bread or white rice.

39

LAMB BURGER

PREP TIME
15 MINS

COOKING TIME
10 MINS

SERVING
6 PERSONS

DIFFICULTY
○ ☑ ○ ○ ○

INGREDIENTS

500G MINCED LAMB
1 RED ONION, DICED
1 – 1.5 TBSP HARISSA SPICE
1 EGG, BEATEN
1 TBSP PLAIN FLOUR
1 HANDFUL OF CORIANDER
LEAVES, CHOPPED
SALT AND PEPPER

PREPARATION

Add the minced lamb, onion, harissa spice, beaten egg, plain flour, coriander leaves and a pinch of salt and pepper to a mixing bowl and mix it with your fingers.

Separate the mixture into 6 portions and start moulding using your hands into burgers. Create a depression in the centre, this will ensure the burgers cook evenly and flat. Place in the fridge to chilled and stiffen.

Grill the burger on the BBQ or shallow fry the burger until thoroughly cooked.

Serve on burger buns with salad and fries.

40

PREPARATION

Mix the minced lamb, onion, garlic, beaten egg, breadcrumbs, chilli flakes, ground coriander, ground cumin, coriander leaves and a pinch of salt and pepper in a bowl. Shape the mixture into small meatballs. Heat the olive oil in a large non-stick frying pan and brown the meatballs. In the same pan, sauté the red onion and garlic for 3-4 minutes until the onion is soft. Add the harissa spices, chilli flakes, ground coriander, ground cumin and tomato puree. Mix well. Add the tomatoes and let the sauce bubble. Turn down the heat and let the sauce simmer for 10 mins. Add the lemon juice and coriander leaves. Season to taste. Add the meatballs into the sauce mixture. Cook for 5 mins and turn off the heat. Serve the meatballs with couscous or pasta.

LAMB MEATBALLS IN MOROCCAN TOMATO SAUCE

PREP TIME
30 MINS

COOKING TIME
30 MINS

SERVING
4 PERSONS

DIFFICULTY
○ ☑ ○ ○ ○

INGREDIENTS

LAMB MEATBALLS
500G MINCED LAMB
1 RED ONION, DICED
2 GARLIC CLOVES, FINELY MINCED
1 EGG, BEATEN
1 TBSP BREADCRUMBS
½ TBSP CHILLI FLAKES (ACCORDING TO TASTE)
2 TSP GROUND CORIANDER
1 TSP GROUND CUMIN
A SMALL BUNCH OF CORIANDER LEAVES, CHOPPED
SALT AND PEPPER
2 TBSP OLIVE OIL

TOMATO SAUCE
1 RED ONION, DICED
2 GARLIC CLOVES, FINELY MINCED
1-2 TBSP HARISSA SPICES
½ TBSP CHILLI FLAKES (ACCORDING TO TASTE)
2 TSP GROUND CORIANDER
1 TSP GROUND CUMIN
½-1 TBSP TOMATO PUREE
1 TIN OF PLUM OR CHOPPED TOMATOES
½ LEMON JUICE
A SMALL BUNCH OF CORIANDER LEAVES, CHOPPED
SALT AND PEPPER

41

SLOW COOKED SAUSAGE, BUTTERNUT SQUASH AND BEAN CASSEROLE

PREP TIME
30 MINS

COOKING TIME
4 (HIGH) - 8 (LOW) HOURS

SERVING
4 PERSONS

DIFFICULTY
○ ✓ ○ ○ ○

INGREDIENTS

2 TBSP OLIVE OIL
12 GOOD QUALITY PORK SAUSAGES
1 LARGE ONION, FINELY CHOPPED
1/BUTTERNUT SQUASH, PEELED, DESEEDED AND CUT INTO CHUNKS
2 TBSP FLOUR
2 TBSP TOMATO PUREE
1 TSP SMOKED PAPRIKA
750ML PORK STOCK
1 HANDFUL OF PARSLEY, CHOPPED
1 TIN OF BUTTER BEANS
1 TIN OF BAKED BEANS IN TOMATO SAUCE
SALT AND PEPPER

PREPARATION

Heat the olive oil, brown the sausages and remove. Use the oil to brown the onions for 2-3 mins. Add the butternut squash, cook for 3-4 mins. Put the butternut squash and onion mixture at the bottom of the slow cooker pot. Sprinkle with half of the flour. Add the butter beans, bake beans, tomato puree, smoked paprika, stock, salt and pepper. Add the rest of the flour. Mix the sauce gently without disturbing the butternut squash and onion mixture. Add the sausages and sprinkle with half of the chopped parsley. Put the slow cooker's lid on. Cook for approximately 4 hours if it's set on high or 8 hours if it is set on low. Stir occasionally. Add the butter beans and baked beans towards the end of the cooking. Season to taste. Once everything is cooked, turn off the slow cooker, garnish with the rest of the chopped parsley and serve.

89

42

SLOW COOKED CHRISTMAS HAM WITH MAPLE SYRUP AND MUSTARD GLAZE

PREP TIME
15 MINS

COOKING TIME
8 HOURS

SERVING
8 PERSONS

DIFFICULTY
○ ○ ✓ ○ ○

INGREDIENTS

2 LARGE ONIONS, CUT INTO TWO
2.5 - 3KG SMOKED OR UNSMOKED GAMMON
8 BLACK PEPPERCORNS
1 CINNAMON STICK
4 BAY LEAVES
4 STAR-ANISES
1 TBSP MIXED SPICE
1L APPLE JUICE
25 WHOLE CLOVES

GLAZE
200ML MAPLE SYRUP
2 TBSP DIJON MUSTARD
2 TBSP WORCESTER SAUCE
2 TBSP SOY SAUCE

PREPARATION

Place the onions at the base of the slow cooker.
Add the gammon and spices and pour the apple juice over the gammon. Slow cook for 8 hrs (low). Heat the oven to 220C/gas 7. Mix all glazing ingredients until smooth. Double line a deep baking tray with foil. Transfer the gammon onto a plate and rest it for few mins to strain the liquid. Remove the skin with a knife leaving a layer of fat on top. Score the fat and stud it with whole cloves. Transfer the gammon onto the baking tray. Mix all glaze ingredients in a bowl. Pour half of the glaze all over the gammon, ensure that the top part is covered. Bake for 25-30 minutes until the gammon. Pour the rest of the glaze onto the gammon halfway through the cooking. Take the gammon out of the oven. Let it rest for 15 mins before carving. Keep the glaze as the sauce.

PASTA, RICE & NOODLES

43

CLASSIC SPAGHETTI WITH TOMATO AND BASIL SAUCE

PREP TIME
5 MINS

COOKING TIME
20 MINS

SERVING
2 PERSONS

DIFFICULTY
○ ☑ ○ ○ ○

INGREDIENTS

1 LARGE WHITE ONION,
QUARTERED
2 CLOVES OF GARLIC
2 FRESH TOMATOES, CHOPPED
1 TBSP OLIVE OIL
1 TIN OF PLUM OR CHOPPED
TOMATOES
2 TBSP TOMATO PUREE
A SMALL BUNCH OF BASIL
LEAVES
SALT AND PEPPER
150G SPAGHETTI, COOKED
ACCORDING TO INSTRUCTIONS

PREPARATION

In a food processor, mix the onion, garlic and fresh tomatoes. In a saucepan, heat the olive oil over medium-high heat. Cook the onion mixture for 3-4 mins. Stir occasionally. Add the tomatoes and tomato puree. Turn down the heat. Cook for another 5 minutes. Season to taste. Add the basil leaves and stir. Add the cooked pasta. Mix well. Turn off the heat and serve with grated cheese and garlic bread.

44

PASTA WITH PRAWNS, CHERRY TOMATOES AND BASIL

PREP TIME
10 MINS

COOKING TIME
10 MINS

SERVING
2 PERSONS

DIFFICULTY
○ ☑ ○ ○ ○

INGREDIENTS

1 TBSP OLIVE OIL

2 GARLIC CLOVES, FINELY MINCED

250G CHERRY TOMATOES, HALVED

100ML WHITE WINE

250G PRAWNS

A SMALL BUNCH OF BASIL LEAVES, CHOPPED

150G PASTA, COOKED ACCORDING TO INSTRUCTIONS

SALT AND PEPPER

PREPARATION

In a large frying pan, sauté the garlic and cherry tomatoes for 3-4 mins until the tomatoes are soft. Add the white wine until it almost evaporates. Add the prawns, cook for 3-4 mins until they are cooked. Season to taste. Add the chopped basil, stir. Finally, add the pasta and mix well. Turn off the heat and serve.

45

SPINACH, MUSHROOM AND RICOTTA CANNELLONI

PREP TIME
30 MINS

COOKING TIME
1 HOUR

SERVING
8 PERSONS

DIFFICULTY
○ ○ ☑ ○ ○

INGREDIENTS

500G RICOTTA CHEESE
250G FROZEN SPINACH, THAWED
250G WHITE OR CHESTNUT
MUSHROOMS, SLICED
SALT AND PEPPER
250G CANNELLONI TUBES
1 TBSP OLIVE OIL
2 LARGE ONIONS, CHOPPED
3 GARLIC CLOVES, CRUSHED
2 BAY LEAVES
2 TIN OF WHOLE OR CHOPPED
TOMATOES
2 TBSP TOMATO PUREE
1 TBSP ITALIAN HERBS
1 TSP GROUND NUTMEG
1/2 TSP GROUND CINNAMON
200G CHEDDAR CHEESE, GRATED OR
MOZZARELLA

PREPARATION

Preheat the oven to 180C/gas 4. In a bowl, mix the ricotta, spinach and mushrooms. Add a pinch of salt and pepper. Fill in each cannelloni tube with the spinach mixture, lay them in a heatproof or casserole dish. Heat the oil in a frying pan over medium heat. Add the onions, garlic and bay leaves. Cook until the onions are tender and fragrant.
Add the tomatoes, tomato puree, Italian herbs, nutmeg and cinnamon. Season to taste.
Cook until the sauce boils, remove from the heat.
Pour the sauce on top of the cannelloni tubes, sprinkle the tubes with the grated cheddar or mozzarella.
Put the dish in the oven, bake for 1 hr or until the cheese is golden.

46

GNOCCHI WITH CHORIZO, PEPPER AND CHERRY TOMATOES

PREP TIME
10 MINS

COOKING TIME
15 MINS

SERVING
2 PERSONS

DIFFICULTY
○ ☑ ○ ○ ○

INGREDIENTS

1 TBSP OLIVE OIL
200G SPANISH CHORIZO, SLICED
2 CLOVES OF GARLIC
1 MEDIUM ONION, CHOPPED
125G CHERRY TOMATOES
1 RED PEPPER (OR ½ RED AND ½ GREEN PEPPERS)
½ TBSP SMOKED PAPRIKA
SALT AND PEPPER
A SMALL BUNCH OF CORIANDER, CHOPPED
500G GNOCCHI, COOK ACCORDING TO INSTRUCTIONS

PREPARATION

Heat the olive oil in a large frying pan. Add the chorizo and cook until the oil comes out. Add the garlic, onion, cherry tomatoes and pepper. Cook until the onion is soft. Add the smoked paprika, stir and season to taste. Stir in the chopped coriander. Turn down the heat and add the cooked gnocchi. Mix well, remove from the heat and serve.

47

BUTTERNUT SQUASH PEARL BARLEY RISOTTO

PREP TIME
20 MINS

COOKING TIME
45 MINS

SERVING
4 PERSONS

DIFFICULTY
○ ✓ ○ ○ ○

INGREDIENTS

1 LARGE ONION, CHOPPED
3 GARLIC CLOVES, FINELY MINCED
1 TBSP OF OLIVE OIL
300G PEARL BARLEY
1 BUTTERNUT SQUASH, PEELED, DESEEDED AND CUBED
150ML WHITE WINE
700ML – 1L VEGETABLE STOCK
SALT AND PEPPER
1 TBSP BUTTER
A SMALL BUNCH OF PARSLEY, CHOPPED

PREPARATION

Sauté the onion and garlic with the olive oil in a large non-stick saucepan. Cook until the onion is soft. Add the pearl barley and butternut squash, coat them in oil. Add the white wine and stir for 5 minutes until the wine evaporates. Add the stock and let it boil. Turn down the heat. Let it simmer for 40-45 mins until the pearl barley and butternut squash are soft and tender, and the sauce thickens. Season to taste. Lastly, stir in the butter and parsley. Remove from the heat and serve.

48

SLOW COOKED BARLEY, PUMPKIN, LEEK AND SAUSAGE CASSEROLE

PREP TIME
20 MINS

COOKING TIME
4 HOURS (HIGH) OR 6 HOURS (LOW)

SERVING
4-6 PERSONS

DIFFICULTY
○ ☑ ○ ○ ○

INGREDIENTS

12 PORK SAUSAGES
2 TBSP OF OLIVE OIL
1 LARGE ONION, CHOPPED
3 GARLIC CLOVES, FINELY MINCED
1-2 TSP ROSEMARY
1-2 TSP THYME
300G PEARL BARLEY
300G PUMPKIN, PEELED, DESEEDED AND CUBED
1 LEEK, SLICED
2 TBSP PLAIN FLOUR
700ML – 1L PORK/CHICKEN STOCK
SALT AND PEPPER

PREPARATION

Brown the sausages in a large frying pan using the olive oil. Remove the sausages. Add the onion, garlic, rosemary and thyme onto the frying pan. Cook until the onion is soft. Add the pearl barley, pumpkin and leek. Occasionally stir and cook for 5 minutes. Remove from the heat. Transfer the barley, leek and pumpkin mix to the slow cooker. Sprinkle with the flour. Add the stock. Mix well. Add the sausages. Slow cook for 6 hours on low or 4 hours on high. 30 minutes before finishing cooking, season to taste.

49

BACON, RADISH AND CHIVE FRIED RICE

PREP TIME
10 MINS

COOKING TIME
10 MINS

SERVING
2 PERSONS

DIFFICULTY
○ ⊘ ○ ○ ○

INGREDIENTS

1 TBSP COOKING OIL
2 EGGS 200G OVERNIGHT RICE,
WARMED IN A MICROWAVE
8 SMOKED BACON, SLICED
2 GARLIC CLOVES, FINELY
CHOPPED
150G PINK RADISHES, SLICED
1 TBSP SESAME OIL
1 TBSP LIGHT SOY SAUCE
SALT AND PEPPER
3 TBSP CHOPPED CHIVES

PREPARATION

Heat the cooking oil a wok over medium heat. Break the eggs in a wok and scramble. Add the bacon, cook for 2 mins. Add the garlic, cook for 1 min. Add the radishes, cook for another 2 mins.
Stir in the rice. Season with the sesame oil, soy sauce, salt and pepper. Stir in the chives and mix well. Transfer to a serving dish and serve.

50

PREPARATION

To make the calamari in spicy basil sauce, blend the garlic, shallots, bird eye chillies in food processor. In a wok or large frying pan, sauté the shallot mixture and the rest of the ingredients (apart from calamari, lemon juice, kecap manis and basil leaves until fragrant and the shallots are soft. Add the calamari and ink, cook for 5 mins. Add the soy sauce and lemon juice. Season to taste. Stir in the basil leaves. Cook for 1 more minute. Remove from the heat and set aside.

INDONESIAN GRILLED RICE WITH CALAMARI
(NASI BAKAR CUMI)

PREP TIME

20 MINS

COOKING TIME

50 MINS

SERVING

4 PERSONS

DIFFICULTY
○ ○ ○ ☑ ○

INGREDIENTS

CALAMARI IN SPICY BASIL SAUCE
3 GARLIC CLOVES
4 SHALLOTS
2 BIRD EYE CHILLIES (ACCORDING TO TASTE)
1 TBSP COOKING OIL
3 LARGE GREEN AND RED CHILLIES
3 SPRING ONIONS, CHOPPED
2 TOMATO, ROUGHLY CHOPPED
2CM GINGER, CRUSHED
2CM GALANGAL, CRUSHED
1 LEMON GRASS, CRUSH THE WHITE AND CUT INTO THREE
5 LIME LEAVES
2 BAY LEAVES
400G CALAMARI, CLEANED, SLICED AND KEEP THE INK
½ LIME OR LEMON JUICE
½ TBSP KECAP MANIS (SWEET SOY SAUCE)

A SMALL BUNCH OF (HOLY) BASIL LEAVES, ROUGHLY CHOPPED
SALT AND PEPPER

SPICED RICE
300G UNCOOKED RICE
600ML WATER
2CM GALANGAL, CRUSHED
1 LEMONGRASS, CRUSH THE WHITE AND CUT INTO THREE
2 BAY LEAVES
6 LIME LEAVES
SALT AND PEPPER
BANANA LEAVES, ENOUGH TO WRAP THE RICE ROLLS
8 TOOTHPICKS
1 TBSP COOKING OIL

51

FISH BALL AND SEAWEED NOODLE SOUP

PREP TIME
3 MINS

COOKING TIME
10 MINS

SERVING
2 PERSONS

DIFFICULTY
☑ ○ ○ ○ ○

INGREDIENTS

2X50G RICE NOODLES, SOAKED IN BOILING WATER FOR 3 MINS AND DRAINED
10 FISH BALLS
30G CHINESE DRY BLACK SEAWEED
1 CLOVE OF GARLIC, CRUSHED
800-900ML WATER OR LIGHT VEGETABLE/CHICKEN/PORK BROTH
1-2 TSP SESAME OIL
A SMALL BUNCH OF CHIVES, CHOPPED
2 TBSP FRIED SHALLOTS

PREPARATION

In a large saucepan, boil the water or broth, garlic and sesame oil. Once it boils, add the fish balls, cook for 3 mins. Season to taste with salt and pepper. Add the seaweed and let it thoroughly wilted. Stir in the rice noodles. Season to taste one more time. Turn off the heat. Divide the soup, noodles and fish balls equally into two bowls. Garnish with chives and fried shallots.

52

Brown the sausages in a large frying pan using the olive oil. Remove the sausages. Add the onion, garlic, rosemary and thyme onto the frying pan. Cook until the onion is soft. Add the pearl barley, pumpkin and leek. Occasionally stir and cook for 5 minutes. Remove from the heat. Transfer the barley, leek and pumpkin mix to the slow cooker. Sprinkle with the flour. Add the stock. Mix well. Add the sausages. Slow cook for 6 hours on low or 4 hours on high. 30 minutes before finishing cooking, season to taste.

PRAWN PAD THAI

PREP TIME
10 MINS

COOKING TIME
15 MINS

SERVING
3-4 PERSONS

DIFFICULTY

○ ☑ ○ ○ ○

INGREDIENTS

300G PAD THAI RICE STICK OR EGG
NOODLES (COOK ACCORDING TO
INSTRUCTION)
200G PRAWNS
2 EGGS
200G BEAN SPROUTS
1 PAK CHOI, SEPARATE THE LEAVES
FROM THE STEMS
4 SHALLOTS, DICED
2 GARLIC, MINCED
2 LARGE CHILLIES, SLICED
3 SPRING ONIONS, CUT INTO 4 PARTS,
SEPARATE THE WHITES AND THE
GREENS
1 TBSP SOY SAUCE (IF DESIRED)

SALT AND PEPPER
3 TBSP COOKING OIL
2 TBSP CRUSHED ROASTED
PEANUTS
1 TBSP CHOPPED CORIANDER
1 LIME, CUT INTO WEDGES
PAD THAI SAUCE
4 TBSP TAMARIND PASTE
4 TBSP FISH SAUCE
4 TBSP GRATED PALM SUGAR

VEGETARIAN &VEGAN

53

CHINESE OMELETTE
(EGG FUYUNG)

PREP TIME
2 MINS

COOKING TIME
5 MINS

SERVING
4 PERSONS

DIFFICULTY

INGREDIENTS

300G CHINESE VEGETABLE STIR FRY MIX

8 EGGS

1 TBSP SOY SAUCE

1 TBSP SHAOXING RICE WINE

½ TBSP SESAME OIL

SALT AND PEPPER

1 TBSP COOKING OIL

2 TBSP SWEET CHILLI SAUCE

PREPARATION

Mix the vegetables, eggs, soy sauce, Shaoxing rice wine, sesame oil, a pinch of salt and pepper in a bowl. Fry the egg mixture in a non-stick frying pan. Cook until the underside is light golden (about 1 1/2 minutes). Flip and cook the other side for 1 minute. Serve with sweet chilli sauce.

54

BROCCOLI, LEEK, POTATO, MUSHROOM AND GREEN PEA PIE

PREP TIME
20 MINS

COOKING TIME
30 MINS

SERVING
6 PERSONS

DIFFICULTY
○ ☑ ○ ○ ○

INGREDIENTS

1 PUFF PASTRY SHEET (YOU CAN ALSO USE SHORTCRUST PASTRY)
4 MEDIUM POTATOES, PEELED AND CUT INTO CHUNKS
2 TBSP BUTTER
1 LARGE ONION, CHOPPED
1 MEDIUM LEEK, SLICED 0.5 CM THICK
2 GARLIC CLOVES, FINELY MINCED
300G BROCCOLI FLORETS
250G MUSHROOMS, SLICED
1 TSP NUTMEG
SALT AND PEPPER
250ML DOUBLE CREAM
150G FROZEN GREEN PEAS
1 TBSP CORNFLOUR, DILUTED WITH 3 TBSP WATER
EGG WASH (1 EGG AND 1 TBSP MILK BEATEN)

PREPARATION

Heat the oven to 200C/gas 6. Boil the potato until soft, drain and set aside. In a large frying pan, melt the butter. Sauté the onion, leek and garlic until fragrant. Add the broccoli, cook until slightly soft. Add the mushrooms and stir. Add the double cream and green peas. Cook until the sauce boils. Add the diluted cornflour, cook until the sauce thickens and season to taste with nutmeg, salt and pepper. Remove from the heat, transfer to a casserole dish. You can do smaller individual pies or one large pie. Cover the dish with the pastry. Before baking, brush the pastry with egg wash.
Bake until crust is golden brown and the mixture is bubbling about 25 to 30 minutes.
Remove from the oven, wait for 5 minutes before serving.

55

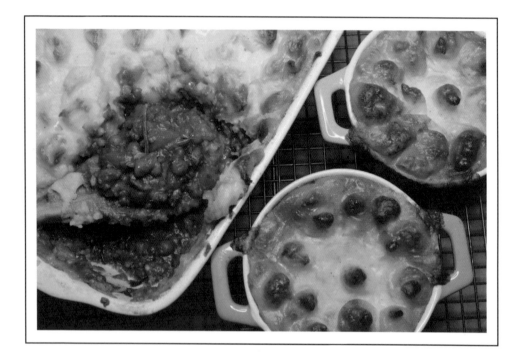

PREPARATION

To make the mince filling, heat the oil in a large frying pan, then soften the onion, garlic, carrots, rosemary and thyme for a few mins. When soft, add the mince and brown. Add the tomato puree and then fry for a few mins. Add the mushrooms and peas, stir. Sprinkle the flour and mix well. Pour over the stock, and cook for 10 mins, occasionally stir. Season to taste. Turn off the heat and set aside.

Heat the oven to 180C/gas 4, then make the mashed potatoes. Boil the potatoes in salted water for 10-15 mins until tender. Drain, then mash with the butter and milk. Season to taste with salt and pepper.

VEGETARIAN SHEPHERD PIE

PREP TIME
15 MINS

COOKING TIME / BAKING TIME
15 MINS / 25 MINS

SERVING
4-5 PERSONS

DIFFICULTY
○ ☑ ○ ○ ○

INGREDIENTS

MINCE FILLING
1 TBSP OLIVE OIL
1 LARGE ONION, CHOPPED
3 CLOVES OF GARLIC, MINCED
2-3 MEDIUM CARROTS, CHOPPED
1 TSP ROSEMARY
1 TSP THYME
500G QUORN MINCE
2 TBSP TOMATO PUREE
200G MUSHROOMS, SLICED
200G FROZEN PEAS
2 TBSP PLAIN FLOUR
500ML VEGETABLE STOCK

MASHED POTATOES
1KG POTATO, PEELED AND CUT INTO CHUNKS
85G BUTTER
3 TBSP MILK
SALT AND PEPPER
1 EGG WASH

56

PREPARATION

To make the chickpea meatballs, heat the oven to 200C/gas 6. In a food processor, whizz the chickpeas, garlic, red onion, coriander leaves, breadcrumbs, chilli powder, salt and pepper. Once everything is mixed, add the egg while the motor is running to bind together. Shape into 18 small balls. Transfer to an oiled baking sheet and cook in the oven for 15 mins, turning halfway.

To make the coconut curry, sauté the onion, garlic, tomatoes and chilli flakes until fragrant and soft in a large wok. Add the garam masala, turmeric, coriander and cumin. Mix well. Add the sweet potatoes. Cook for 4-5 mins. Make sure that everything is covered in oil. Cook for 2 mins. Add the coconut milk. Let it boil then simmer until the sweet potatoes are tender. Add the chickpea meatballs and spinach. Season to taste. Stir in the coriander leaves. Turn off the heat and serve with basmati rice.

CHICKPEA MEATBALL CURRY

PREP TIME
10 MINS.

COOKING TIME
45 MINS.

SERVING
4 PERSONS

DIFFICULTY
○ ○ ✓ ○ ○

INGREDIENTS

CHICKPEA MEATBALLS
1 TIN OF CHICKPEAS, DRAINED
3 GARLIC CLOVES
1 LARGE RED ONION
A SMALL BUNCH OF CORIANDER
LEAVES
1 EGG, BEATEN (VEGAN - USE FLAX
EGG: MIX 1TBSP GROUND FLAXSEED
WITH 3 TBSP WATER, LEAVE IT IN THE
FRIDGE FOR 15 MINS TO THICKEN)
½ TSP CHILLI POWDER (ACCORDING
TO TASTE)
2-3 TBSP BREADCRUMBS
SALT AND PEPPER
½ TBSP OLIVE OIL

COCONUT CURRY
1 TBSP OLIVE OIL
1 LARGE ONION, CHOPPED
3 CLOVES OF GARLIC
2 TOMATOES, CUT INTO CHUNKS
1 TBSP CHILLI FLAKES
1-2 TBSP GARAM MASALA
1/2 - 1 TBSP GROUND TURMERIC
1-2 TSP GROUND CORIANDER
1/2 - 1 TSP GROUND CUMIN
2 SWEET POTATOES, PEELED AND CUT
INTO CHUNKS
3 HANDFUL OF SPINACH
SALT AND PEPPER
1 SMALL BUNCH OF CORIANDER LEAVES,
CHOPPED

57

INDONESIAN TOFU CURRY
(KARE TAHU)

PREP TIME
20 MINS

COOKING TIME
15 MINS

SERVING
4-6 PERSONS

DIFFICULTY
○ ☑ ○ ○ ○

INGREDIENTS

1 RED ONION, QUARTERED
4 CLOVES OF GARLIC
2-3 LARGE RED CHILLIES, CHOPPED
4 KEMIRI OR MACADAMIA NUTS, SLIGHTLY ROASTED
2 TBSP COOKING OIL
1 LEMONGRASS, CRUSH THE WHITE PART AND CUT IT INTO THREE
2CM GALANGAL, CRUSHED
2CM GINGER, CRUSHED
4 LIME LEAVES
1 TBSP GROUND CORIANDER
1 TBSP GROUND TURMERIC
½ TBSP GROUND CUMIN
1 TIN OF COCONUT MILK
SALT AND PEPPER
600G TOFU, CUT INTO TRIANGLES OR CUBED, AND FRIED
1 TBSP OF FRIED ONIONS

PREPARATION

In a food processor, blend the red onion, garlic, red chillies, roasted kemiri/macadamia nuts and 1 tbsp of cooking oil until smooth. In a wok, heat the remaining oil over medium-high heat. Add the curry paste, lemongrass, galangal, ginger and lime leaves. Cook for 5 minutes. Keep stirring so that the paste does not stick on the bottom of the pan. Add the ground coriander, turmeric and cumin. Mix well and cook for another 2-3 minutes. Make sure that the paste is cooked. Add the coconut milk and bring to boil. If a little thick, add a little bit of water. Season to taste. Add the tofu into the wok. Cook for another 2 minutes. Remove from the heat and transfer to a bowl. Sprinkle with the fried onions.

58

ROASTED MASALA VEGETABLES

PREP TIME
10 MINS

COOKING TIME
30 MINS

SERVING
3-4 PERSONS

DIFFICULTY
☑ ○ ○ ○ ○

INGREDIENTS

3-4 TBSP OLIVE OIL
1 TBSP GARAM MASALA
1 TBSP GROUND CORIANDER
1/2 TBSP GROUND CUMIN
1/2 TBSP CHILLI FLAKES
(ACCORDING TO TASTE)
SALT AND PEPPER
1 AUBERGINE, CUBED
1 SWEET POTATO, PEELED CUBED
1/2 BUTTERNUT SQUASH, PEELED
AND CUBED
2 PEPPERS, SLICED
2 GARLIC CLOVES, FINELY MINCED
1/2 LIME OR LEMON JUICE
1 SMALL HANDFUL OF CORIANDER
LEAVES, CHOPPED

PREPARATION

Heat the oven to 200C/gas 6.
In a bowl mix the olive oil with the garam masala, coriander, cumin and chilli flakes. Season with salt and pepper.
Put all vegetables in a baking tray, drizzle with the oil mixture and mix well.
Put the tray in the oven, cook for 30 mins or until the vegetables are tender. Turn the vegetables halfway through to the cooking.
Once cooked, remove from the oven.
Squeeze the lime or lemon juice over the vegetables. Sprinkle with the coriander leaves. Mix well and serve.

59

PREPARATION

Preheat the oven to 200C/gas 6. Parboil the potatoes and drain. Put the potatoes in a roasting tray, drizzle with 1 tbsp olive oil and season with salt and pepper, place the tray on the upper rack of the oven for 30 to 40 minutes, or until golden and tender. When the potatoes and vegetables are done roasting, remove from the oven and reduce oven temperature to 180C/gas 4.

Put the courgettes and aubergine in another roasting tray, drizzle with 1 tbsp olive oil and season with salt and pepper. Place the tin on the lower rack of the oven, roast for 40 minutes until the vegetables are tender and roasted.
Toss the potatoes and vegetables occasionally so they are equally cooked.
Put 1 tbsp olive oil into a frying pan, sauté the onion, garlic bay leaves, for about 2 minutes until the onion is soft. Add sliced peppers and cook for 1 min.

VEGETARIAN MOUSSAKA

PREP TIME
2 HOURS

COOKING TIME
1 HOUR

SERVING
6-8 PERSONS

DIFFICULTY
○ ○ ○ ✓ ○

INGREDIENTS

3 LARGE POTATOES, PEELED AND CUT INTO 1CM THICK
2 TBSP OLIVE OIL
2 COURGETTES, CUT INTO 0.5CM THICK
1 AUBERGINE, PEELED, CREATE A STRIPE EFFECT AND CUT INTO 0.5CM THICK
150G GRATED CHEDDAR
SALT AND PEPPER

TOMATO MIXTURE:
2 MIXED PEPPERS, SLICED
3 CLOVES GARLIC, PEELED AND MINCED
1 LARGE ONION, DICED
4 BAY LEAVES

1 TIN OF CHICKPEAS
3 MIXED PEPPERS, SLICED
1 TIN OF CHICKPEAS
2 TINS OF PLUM TOMATOES
1 TBSP ITALIAN HERBS
1/2 TSP CINNAMON
1/2 TSP CHILLI FLAKES

BÉCHAMEL SAUCE:
700ML MILK
1 EGG, BEATEN
1 BAY LEAVE
A PINCH OF NUTMEG
A PINCH OF PEPPER
50G UNSALTED BUTTER
3 TBSP PLAIN FLOUR

60

MOROCCAN CHICKPEA, SWEET POTATO AND KIDNEY BEAN STEW

PREP TIME
15 MINS

COOKING TIME
20 MINS

SERVING
8 PERSONS

DIFFICULTY
○ ☑ ○ ○ ○

INGREDIENTS

1 TBSP OLIVE OIL
1 LARGE ONION, DICED
3 GARLIC CLOVES, MINCED
1/2 TBSP CHILLI FLAKES (ACCORDING TO TASTE)
2 TOMATOES, CHOPPED
3 BAY LEAVES
1 TBSP TOMATO PUREE
2 TBSP HARISSA SPICES
1 TBSP PAPRIKA
2 MEDIUM SWEET POTATOES, PEELED AND CUBED
2 RED PEPPERS, CHOPPED
2 TINS CHOPPED OR WHOLE TOMATOES
2 TINS CHICKPEAS, DRAINED
1 TIN KIDNEY BEANS, DRAINED
SALT AND PEPPER
A SMALL BUNCH OF CORIANDER LEAVES, CHOPPED

PREPARATION

Heat the olive oil in a wok or a large frying pan over medium heat. Add the onion, garlic, chilli flakes, tomatoes and bay leaves. Cook until fragrant. Add the tomato puree, harissa spices and paprika. Mix well. Add the sweet potatoes and peppers. Add the chopped or whole tomatoes. Cook until the sweet potatoes are quite soft (approx. 10 mins). Add the chickpeas and kidney beans. Stir and season to taste. Cook for further 5 mins. Add the coriander leaves, mix well. Remove from the heat and transfer to a serving dish. Serve the stew with couscous or a mixture of couscous and quinoa.

61

SLOW COOKED VEGETARIAN CHILLI

PREP TIME
10 MINS

COOKING TIME
3 HOURS (HIGH) OR 6 HOURS (LOW)

SERVING
4 PERSONS

DIFFICULTY

INGREDIENTS

350G QUORN MINCE
1 DICED ONION
3 CLOVES OF MINCED GARLIC,
3 CARROT, PEELED AND SLICED
2 MIXED PEPPERS, ROUGHLY CHOPPED
1 TIN OF RED KIDNEY BEANS
1 LEEK, DICED
1 TIN OF CHOPPED TOMATOES
3 TBSP TOMATO PUREE
1-2 TBSP PAPRIKA POWDER
1 TBSP GROUND CORIANDER
1/2-1 TBSP GROUND CUMIN
SALT AND PEPPER
A SMALL BUNCH OF CORIANDER LEAVES, CHOPPED

PREPARATION

Put all ingredients into a slow cooker and cook for 3 hours (high) or 6 hours (low): 1 hour before finishing cooking, stir, season to taste, and add 1 tin of red kidney beans. Once cooked, serve with boiled long grain rice and sprinkle with chopped coriander leaves.

62

PREPARATION

Divide the rice noodles in bowls. In a food processor blend the laksa paste ingredients until smooth. Sauté the paste, peanut butter, ground coriander, cumin and turmeric in a large wok for 3-4 minutes until fragrant, make sure that it doesn't burn. Add the sweet potato and cauliflower florets, coat in oil. Add the coconut milk. Cook for 2 minutes. Add the peppers and aubergine. When everything is almost soft, add the courgette. When the sauce is too thick add some water. Let the sauce bubbles and season to taste. Remove from the heat and pour over the laksa over the rice noodle. Garnish with coriander leaves.

VEGAN LAKSA

PREP TIME
20 MINS

COOKING TIME
20 MINS

SERVING
6 PERSONS

DIFFICULTY

○ ⊘ ○ ○ ○

INGREDIENTS

6 X 50G RICE NOODLES, SOAKED IN HOT WATER AND DRAINED
1 SWEET POTATO, PEELED AND CUBED
100G CAULIFLOWER FLORETS
2 TINS OF COCONUT MILK
1 RED PEPPER
1 GREEN PEPPER
1 AUBERGINE, CUBED
1 COURGETTE, CUBED
150G FRIED TOFU
1 TBSP PEANUT BUTTER (OPTIONAL)
2 TBSP GROUND CORIANDER
½ TBSP GROUND CUMIN

1 TBSP GROUND TURMERIC
1 TBSP COOKING OIL
SALT AND PEPPER

LAKSA PASTE
2-3 LARGE CHILLIES, CUT INTO LARGE PIECES (ACCORDING TO TASTE)
2 LEMONGRASS STALKS, CHOPPED
2CM GALANGAL, CHOPPED
4 SHALLOTS, QUARTERED
3 GARLIC CLOVES
4 LIME LEAVES
1 LIME JUICE
A SMALL BUNCH OF CORIANDER STALKS, KEEP THE LEAVES FOR GARNISH

DESSERTS & CAKES

63 | SPICED CHOCOLATE PANNA COTTA

DIFFICULTY	PREP TIME	COOKING TIME	CHILL	SERVING
○ ⊘ ○ ○ ○	10 MINS	30 MINS	5-6 HOURS OVERNIGHT	4 PERSONS

INGREDIENTS

1 PACKET OF VEGE-GEL

200ML COLD WATER

250ML DOUBLE CREAM

120ML WHOLE MILK

1 TSP MIXED SPICE

1 CINNAMON STICK OR 1/2 TSP GROUND CINNAMON

80G CASTER SUGAR

100G DARK CHOCOLATE, ROUGHLY CHOPPED

1 TSP OF VANILLA EXTRACT

1 TSP CACAO POWDER

PREPARATION

Prepare 4 ramekins/jars/glasses. Dissolve the sachet of the Vege-Gel into the cold water. Mix the double cream, milk, mixed spice, cinnamon stick (or ground cinnamon) and sugar and heat the mixture over medium heat until it begins to boil. Turn off the heat and add the chopped chocolates and vanilla extract. Hand whisk the mixture until completely incorporated. Stir in the Vege-Gel mixture and heat it until almost boils. Remove the cinnamon stick. Chill in the fridge for 5-6 hours or overnight. Sprinkle with cacao powder before serving.

64 | LEMON POSSET AND LEMON AND GINGER SHORTBREAD

DIFFICULTY	PREP TIME	COOKING TIME	SERVING
○ ✓ ○ ○ ○	40 MINS	30 MINS	4-6 PERSONS

INGREDIENTS

LEMON POSSET
150G CASTER SUGAR
2 LEMON JUICE AND ZEST
600ML DOUBLE CREAM
A PINCH OF NUTMEG
A PINCH OF GINGER

LEMON AND GINGER SHORTBREAD
PREP 30 MINS; BAKE 20 MINS

INGREDIENTS
125G BUTTER
55G CASTER SUGAR, PLUS EXTRA TO FINISH
250G PLAIN FLOUR
1 TSP GROUND GINGER
A PINCH OF GROUND NUTMEG
1 LEMON JUICE AND ZEST

PREPARATION

Lemon posset
In a large saucepan bring the sugar and lemon juice and zest to boil until the sugar is dissolved. Set aside and keep warm. In another saucepan bring to boil the double cream, nutmeg and ginger. Pour the cream into the sugar and lemon mixture. Mix well. Sift through the mixture into a jug. Divide the mixture into 4-6 ramekins. Let it cool and refrigerate for 3 hours until they set.

Lemon and ginger shortbread
Heat the oven to 190C/Gas 5.
Beat the butter and the sugar together until smooth.
Sift in and fold the flour, ginger and nutmeg into the mixture.
Stir in the lemon juice and zest and form a dough. Turn on to a work surface and gently roll out the dough until 1cm or ½ inch thick.
Cut into rounds or fingers and place onto a baking tray. Sprinkle with caster sugar and chill in the fridge for 20 minutes.
Bake in the oven for 15-20 minutes, or until pale golden-brown. Set aside to cool on a wire rack.

Serve the lemon posset with lemon and ginger biscuits.

65 | MATCHA ICE CREAM

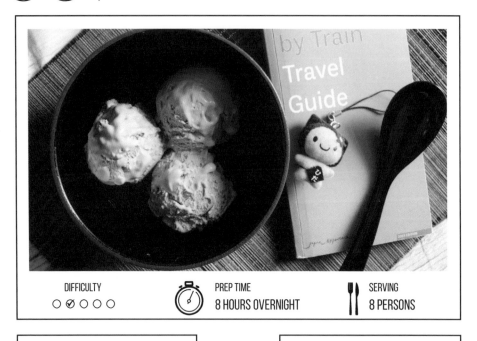

DIFFICULTY
○ ⊘ ○ ○ ○

PREP TIME
8 HOURS OVERNIGHT

SERVING
8 PERSONS

INGREDIENTS

3 TBSP MATCHA (GREEN TEA) POWDER
250ML FULL-FAT MILK
500ML DOUBLE CREAM
150G CASTER SUGAR
3 EGGS

PREPARATION

Sift the matcha powder into a bowl to remove any lumps. Add 3 tbsp of milk and whisk until the matcha powder is dissolved. Mix the remaining milk into the mixture. In a large saucepan, mix the double cream and matcha mixture. Cook the mixture over medium-low heat for 5 minutes until heated through, and stir occasionally. Remove from the heat.

Whisk the sugar and eggs in a bowl. Pour 1/3 of the matcha mixture into the bowl and mix thoroughly. Mix in the rest of the matcha mixture. Transfer the mixture back into the pot and cook over medium-low heat for about 3 minutes. Remove from the heat and cool to room temperature. Refrigerate for at least two hours until the mixture is completely cooled. Whisk again before churning the mixture. Churn the mixture according to the ice cream maker instruction. Pour the ice cream into an airtight container. Freeze for at least two hours or overnight.

66 | CHRISTMAS TRIFLE

DIFFICULTY
○ ⊘ ○ ○ ○

PREP TIME
6 HOURS

SERVING
6 PERSONS

INGREDIENTS

250G SPONGE CAKE OR STRAWBERRY
SWISS ROLL
100G FROZEN BERRIES
135G STRAWBERRY JELLY CUBES (I
USED HARTLEY'S)
3 TBSP CHOCOLATE FLAKES OR
SHREDDED CHOCOLATE

CUSTARD
2 TBSP CASTER SUGAR
3 TBSP CORNFLOUR
3 EGG YOLKS
600ML MILK
½ - 1 TBSP VANILLA ESSENCE

WHIPPED CREAM
250ML DOUBLE CREAM
2 TBSP ICING SUGAR
1 TBSP VANILLA ESSENCE

PREPARATION

Cover the base of a large bowl or jars with pieces of sponge cake or Swiss roll (1.5 thickness). Layer with the frozen fruits and set aside. Make the jelly according to instructions. Pour the jelly over the fruits (1.5cm thickness). You may not need to use all the jelly. Let it cool and put it in the fridge for 2-3 hours to set.

In the meantime, make the custard. In a bowl, mix the sugar, cornflour and egg yolks until smooth. Heat the milk until just boiling. Pour the milk over the egg mixture and whisk until smooth. Strain the mixture into a clean saucepan. Stir constantly and cook gently until the custard thickens. Stir in the vanilla essence. Cover the custard with cling film and let it cool. Once the jelly is set and the custard is cool, make the whipped cream.

In a bowl, whisk the double cream, icing sugar and vanilla essence on high speed until it reaches stiff peaks.

To assemble the trifle, cover the jelly with the custard (1.5cm thickness). Cover the custard with the whipped cream (1.5cm thickness) and sprinkle the chocolate flakes or shredded chocolate on top of the cream. Refrigerate for at least 2 hrs.

141

67 | PORTUGUESE CUSTARD TARTS (PASTÉIS DE NATA)

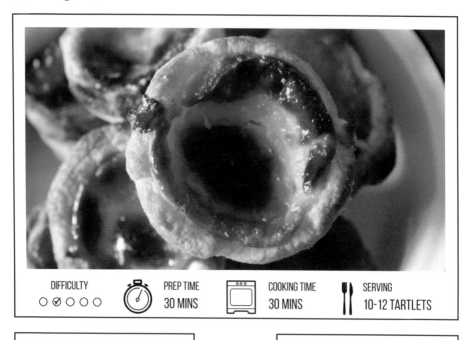

DIFFICULTY	PREP TIME	COOKING TIME	SERVING
○ ✓ ○ ○ ○	30 MINS	30 MINS	10-12 TARTLETS

INGREDIENTS

COOKING SPRAY

1 LARGE WHOLE EGG

2 LARGE EGG YOLKS

115G GOLDEN CASTER SUGAR

2 TBSP CORNFLOUR

400ML FULL FAT MILK

1 CINNAMON STICK

2 TSP VANILLA EXTRACT

1 SHEET READY ROLLED PUFF PASTRY

1 TSP ICING SUGAR

PREPARATION

Lightly grease a 12-hole muffin tin with the cooking spray. Pre-heat the oven to 200C/Gas 6. Mix the egg, yolks, sugar and cornflour in a pan. Gradually add the milk until mixture is well mixed and smooth. Add the cinnamon stick.

Heat the mixture over medium heat. Stir constantly until the mixture thickens and comes to the boil. Remove the pan from heat, stir in the vanilla extract and remove the cinnamon stick.

Put the custard in a glass bowl to cool and cover with cling film to prevent skin forming.

Cut the pastry sheet into two pieces, sprinkle icing sugar on one piece, and place them on top of each other. Roll the pastry tightly, from the short side, into a log and cut the log into 12 even sized rounds.

On a lightly floured board, roll each round into a disc (approx. 10cm) and press the pastry discs into the muffin tin.

Spoon in the cooled custard and bake for 25-30 mins until golden on top. Leave to cool in the tin for 5mins then move to a cooling rack to finish cooling although they can be eaten warm.

68 | BAILEYS BROWNIES

DIFFICULTY
○ ⊘ ○ ○ ○

PREP TIME
10 MINS

COOKING TIME
20 MINS

SERVING
18 SLICES

INGREDIENTS

120ML VEGETABLE OIL

225G CUP CASTER SUGAR

1 TBSP COFFEE DILUTED WITH 50ML WATER, LET IT COOL

50ML BAILEYS

2 LARGE EGGS

1 TSP VANILLA

1/4 TSP BAKING POWDER

50G COCOA POWDER

1/4 TSP SALT

75G FLOUR

100G WHITE CHOCOLATE CHIP

PREPARATION

Preheat the oven to 180C/gas 4.

Mix the oil, sugar, coffee and baileys until well blended.

Add the eggs and vanilla, stir until just blended.

Sift the flour, baking powder, cocoa powder and salt into the egg mixture. Add the white chocolate chip. Mix until just blended.

Pour the mixture into greased 20×28cm baking tin or smaller.

Bake for 20 minutes or until the sides just start to pull away from the pan.

Cool completely before cutting.

69 | SPICED PUMPKIN CUPCAKES WITH CINNAMON BUTTERCREAM

DIFFICULTY	PREP TIME	BAKING TIME	SERVING
○ ○ ⊘ ○ ○	30 MINS	25 MINS	24 PIECES

INGREDIENTS

SPICED PUMPKIN CUPCAKES
300G PLAIN FLOUR
2 TBSP MIXED SPICE
125G BUTTER, SOFTENED
125G WHITE SUGAR
75G BROWN SUGAR
2 EGGS
180ML MILK
225G PUMPKIN PUREE (CUT A PUMPKIN INTO
QUARTERS, THEN PEEL AND CUT INTO CHUNKS.
BOIL THE PUMPKIN FOR 20 MINS UNTIL TENDER,
DRAIN AND ALLOW TO COOL. PUREE THE FLESH
IN A FOOD PROCESSOR).
1 TSP BAKING POWDER
1/2 TSP BAKING SODA

CINNAMON BUTTERCREAM
250G BUTTER
250G ICING SUGAR
2-3 TSP GROUND CINNAMON
2-3 TSP VANILLA EXTRACT
2-3 TBSP MILK

PREPARATION

To make the spiced pumpkin cupcakes, preheat the oven to 200C/gas 6. Grease 24 muffin cups, or line with paper muffin liners. Sift together the flour and the mixed spice set aside.

Beat the butter, white sugar and brown sugar with an electric mixer in a large bowl until light and fluffy. Add one egg at a time, allowing each egg to blend into the butter mixture before adding the next. Stir in the milk and pumpkin puree after the last egg. Stir in the flour mixture, mixing until just incorporated. Pour the batter into the prepared muffin cups.

Bake in the preheated oven until golden and the tops spring back when lightly pressed, about 25 minutes. Cool in the pans for 5 minutes before removing to cool completely on a wire rack.

To make the cinnamon buttercream, cream the butter with an electric whisk. Sift in half of the icing sugar and ground cinnamon, beat until smooth. Add the remaining icing sugar, vanilla and milk, add more milk if necessary. Beat until the mixture is smooth and creamy. Once the cupcakes are cool, frost the cupcakes with the buttercream icing.

70 | GLAZED CHERRY LOAF CAKE

DIFFICULTY	PREP TIME	BAKING TIME	SERVING
○ ⊘ ○ ○ ○	20 MINS	45 MINS	10 - 12 SLICES

INGREDIENTS

230G BUTTER

300G CASTER SUGAR

4 EGGS, BEATEN

1 TBSP VANILLA ESSENCE

250G FLOUR

1 TSP BAKING POWDER

300G GLAZED CHERRIES, CHOPPED

1 TSP ICING SUGAR FOR DUSTING

PREPARATION

Preheat the oven to 180C/gas 4.

Cream the butter and sugar until fluffy. Gradually add the beaten eggs and vanilla, mix well.

Sift the flour and baking powder together into the egg mixture. Fold the flour into the mixture carefully and add the chopped cherries. Mix one more time.

Pour the batter into a lined loaf tin. Bake for 45-50 mins. Insert a skewer into the centre, if it comes out clean, the cake is done. Remove from the oven and allow to cool completely in the tin. Dust with the icing sugar before serving.